Translation Practices Explained

Translation Practices Explained is a series of coursebooks designed to help self-learners and teachers of translation. Each volume focuses on a specific aspect of professional translation practice, in many cases corresponding to actual courses available in translator-training institutions. Special volumes are devoted to well consolidated professional areas, such as legal translation or European Union texts; to areas where labour-market demands are currently undergoing considerable growth, such as screen translation in its different forms; and to specific aspects of professional practices on which little teaching and learning material is available, the case of editing and revising, or electronic tools. The authors are practising translators or translator trainers in the fields concerned. Although specialists, they explain their professional insights in a manner accessible to the wider learning public.

These books start from the recognition that professional translation practices require something more than elaborate abstraction or fixed methodologies. They are located close to work on authentic texts, and encourage learners to proceed inductively, solving problems as they arise from examples and case studies.

Each volume includes activities and exercises designed to help self-learners consolidate their knowledge; teachers may also find these useful for direct application in class, or alternatively as the basis for the design and preparation of their own material. Updated reading lists and website addresses will also help individual learners gain further insight into the realities of professional practice.

Dorothy Kelly
Series Editor

Note-taking
for Consecutive Interpreting

A Short Course

Andrew Gillies

St. Jerome Publishing
Manchester, UK & Kinderhook (NY), USA

Published by

St. Jerome Publishing
2 Maple Road West, Brooklands
Manchester, M23 9HH, United Kingdom
Telephone +44 (0)161 973 9856
Fax +44 (0)161 905 3498
ken@stjeromepublishing.com
http://www.stjerome.co.uk

InTrans Publications
P. O. Box 467
Kinderhook, NY 12106, USA
Telephone (518) 758-1755
Fax (518) 758-6702

ISBN 1-900650-82-7 (pbk)
ISSN 1470-966X (*Translation Practices Explained*)

British Library Cataloguing in Publication Data
A catalogue record of this book is available from the British Library

Library of Congress Cataloging-in-Publication Data
Gillies, Andrew, 1971-
Note-taking for consecutive interpreting : a short course / Andrew Gillies.
      p. cm. -- (Translation practices explained)
Includes bibliographical references.
ISBN 1-900650-82-7 (pbk. : alk. paper)
1. Translating and interpreting. 2. Note-taking. I. Title. II. Series.
P306.2.G58 2005
418'.02--dc22

2005017809

More often than not, the "greats" will tell you that consecutive interpretation cannot be learnt and that note-taking depends upon the personality of the interpreter. I am afraid my own experience shows otherwise. If the fundamentals [...] are in place then note-taking can easily be learnt.

Rozan, 2003:11 [1956:9]

The oft repeated argument that notes are an entirely personal affair, and the implicit suggestion that they cannot therefore be taught, does not hold water.

Andres, 2000:58

Contents

Part I   The Basics Step-by-step

Acknowledgements

Thanks to: David Walker and Brian Huebner for really knowing what consecutive interpreting is about; Guy Laycock for his invaluable contribution; Andrew Marson, Nick Woodman and Jasper Tilbury for their help in reading and checking the drafts; to Dorothy Kelly as editor; to Tatiana for all her support and help; and all the colleagues and students who took part in the Cracow interpreting workshops 2001-04.

PART I

The Basics Step-by-step

...if we are to teach, we must teach something, and that something must be simple and methodical.

Rozan, 2003:11 [1956:9]

Introduction

What is consecutive interpreting?

Consecutive interpreting is one of the two skills that go to make up what we call conference interpreting. It involves listening to what someone has to say and then, when they have finished, reproducing the same message in another language. The speech may be anything between a minute and twenty minutes in length and the interpreter will rely on a combination of notes, memory and general knowledge to recreate their version of the original. A speaker, an interpreter, a notepad[§] and a pen is all the equipment you will need.

When is consecutive interpreting used?

Seventy years ago conference interpreting meant consecutive interpreting. Simultaneous interpreting, or the equipment to make it possible, had not yet been invented and consecutive interpreting was the standard for international meetings of every kind. Simultaneous interpreting came along after World War II and by the 1970s had overtaken consecutive as the main form of conference interpretation.

Consecutive interpreting has not disappeared, however. It is still an essential part of an interpreter's repertoire and is considered by many to be the superior of the two skills. Indeed on the free market it is also better paid! Although simultaneous interpreting has replaced consecutive almost entirely at the meeting room table, where conference facilities are often able to supply the equipment required to provide simultaneous interpreting, there are many situations where consecutive survives and will continue to survive.

Ceremonial speeches

There are many occasions where a speaker makes a formal speech that needs then to be interpreted consecutively. After-dinner speeches at banquets or to open receptions are a classic example: the host will want to say a few words to the guests and the guests will want to reply. You, the interpreter(s), are there to facilitate that. You may also find that you have been recruited to interpret for the opening of a cultural event held at a centre like the British Council or Goethe Institute. The organizer will introduce the event in, say, English or German and you will interpret into the language of the host country. There is no real limit on the type of ceremonial speech you will be asked to interpret. It could be the opening of a French supermarket in Poland, or the launch of a German boat in Korea. It could be a foreign winner of an award making an acceptance speech in their own language, or a composer's 70th birthday at the Philharmonic.

Visits and guided tours

Groups of MPs, business people, technical experts and more besides will often make trips abroad as part of their jobs. Often these visits will involve seeing how things work in another country. This means getting out of the fully equipped conference centre and off into consecutive country. If your clients have come to see a certain industrial process then you may be bussed off to a plant where it is used and expected to interpret consecutively the explanations offered by a knowledgeable guide of how it all works. Alternatively, if you are accompanying a group of agricultural experts you can expect to find yourself down on the farm for a round or two of consecutive. There is no end to the type of place you may visit. Slaughterhouses, pharmaceutical production units, fish-filleting plants and furniture factories. You name it and one of our colleagues has already been there and worked in consecutive mode[§].

Visiting groups also have social programmes arranged for them in the evenings or on the free afternoon at the end of the trip. So when you get back from the slaughterhouse you may well find yourself interpreting consecutively what a tourist guide has to say about the local sights and attractions; the owner of a local brewery as he introduces you to his products; or the host of the visit wishing everyone a pleasant meal and opening the buffet.

Working meetings without equipment

Sometimes of course, you will still find yourself in an old-fashioned meeting room, interpreting consecutively what the participants have to say to one another across the table. The meeting rooms will all look much the same, but the subject of the debate will depend on who your clients are.

Accreditation tests

Finally, it is worth mentioning accreditation tests. Many large international institutions insist on testing interpreters' abilities before offering them any work. Such accreditation tests cannot be considered to be "real" interpreting: we are not helping people with no mutual language to communicate with one another. Rather we are demonstrating to people who understand perfectly the two languages involved that we are capable of facilitating that communication when necessary. But, if you are reading this book, then at some stage in your future career you are very likely to take such a test. Consecutive interpreting is an integral part of most accreditation tests, and more often than not it is the first part and it is eliminatory. In other words, if you fail it you won't even be asked to take a test of your simultaneous skills. This is one of many good reasons to put time and effort into improving your consecutive interpreting skills.

About this book

Back in the 1950s and 60s there were a couple of legendary interpreters who could reproduce speeches of twenty and thirty minutes from memory. Those of us with more modest abilities - and that includes every interpreter working today - rely on a combination of memory, general knowledge and notes to do the same. This book looks at those notes because, like it or not, you will have to take notes when interpreting consecutively and the way you take those notes will have an enormous impact on the success of your interpretation. Not knowing how to take notes, and the detrimental effect that that will have on your performance interpreting could discourage you from joining the profession before you even really get started. Alternatively, once you finish your training and start working, poorly thought-out notes will stop you from reaching your full potential as an interpreter. This workbook aims to help student interpreters to work progressively towards a system for note-taking in consecutive interpreting which is consistent, simple to learn, adaptable and efficient. A system which, when practised and ingrained, will help interpreters to interpret better in consecutive mode by saving time and intellectual effort, and by offering consistent solutions to frequently occurring problems.

Parts I - III

The book assumes a general understanding of what consecutive interpreting is, and also that most readers will be involved in, or have been involved in, some kind of formal interpreter training, although this is not a prerequisite for using this book. The book is split into three parts. Part I is a step-by-step introduction to this note-taking system and takes the reader through a series of stages towards a framework system of consecutive notes. One chapter is devoted to each stage, and each stage should be practised in isolation and mastered before moving on to the next. Each subsequent chapter builds on the techniques learnt in the previous one. This note-taking system forms a self-contained whole but can and should be adapted and built upon as each interpreter sees fit. Practice ideas are explained at the end of each chapter. The basic structure of each chapter will be as follows:

- Guidelines for using a technique
- Example of the use of that technique
- Practice task for student
- Example of how the task might have been completed (to be found at the back of the book in Part III)
- Tips on further practice

Part II is a collection of tips and ideas which are not an integral part of the system but which can be used within it and which have been tried and tested successfully by many interpreters. This part of the book expands on some of the techniques described in Part I as well as offering a few additional ideas. You can consult these whenever you feel the need or curiosity inspires you. The sections in Part II are self-contained.

In Part III you will find a series of sample speeches, notes taken from them and commentaries on those notes, together with versions of the tasks set in Part I, information about the examples used in Parts I and II, and tips on how and where to find more practice material.

Finally, you will find a glossary of terms used recommendations on further reading, and the complete list of references. The terms which appear in the glossary are highlighted at first mention with the symbol [§].

Note-taking for consecutive interpreting

There are several reasons why having a considered and consistent system for taking notes in consecutive interpreting is useful, if not essential, and these ideas are described below.

Macro-thinking[§]

In economics micro- means looking at the individual, the small scale, whereas macro- means examining the workings of the whole national or international economy. Here too, macro- means looking at the bigger picture. Whereas words, expressions and ideas are part of the micro-level, the structure, framework and way the speech is built up form the macro-level.

Notes taken in consecutive interpreting are a representation of the skeleton structure of the speech. **The original speech is a group of ideas in a certain order;** it is not an arbitrary muddle of unrelated ideas. In the speaker's mind at least, the ideas that make up a speech are related to one another, be it logically, chronologically, or by their relative importance. These relationships and the structures used to express them are limited in number and occur repeatedly in all sorts of speeches, so once you have learnt to recognize them you will need a quick and consistent way of noting them. In this way **your notes become the visual representation of your analysis of the source speech[§].** The notes must be at least as clear as the analysis preceding them, otherwise the analysis is wasted, and usually the notes will be clearer in structure than the original speech, so that the interpreter can easily transmit the same message to the audience.

You will be listening at two levels: to the words of the speech in order to understand them, but also to the overall speech, to how the bits fit together. This is what we mean by a macro-approach[§]. It is the focus of Chapter 1 in particular but also underlies the ideas in Chapters 3, 4, 5 and in Part II, Other uses of the Margin.

Capacity

Consecutive interpreting involves a number of different tasks that have to be completed at the same time with finite and competing intellectual capacities - multi-tasking[§]. Gile (1995:178) outlines these tasks as follows,

Phase 1:   listening and analysis, note-taking, short-term memory operations, coordination of these tasks

Phase 2:   note-reading, remembering, production[§]

In Phase 1 the most common problem for student interpreters (but also experienced interpreters) is that it is difficult to do all these things at the same time. We have finite intellectual capacity. For example, **if you are thinking too much about how to note something, you will listen less well.** In fact not hearing something is much more common among student interpreters than not understanding something. You do not hear because you are concentrating too much on deciphering the original or on taking notes. The overload makes you deaf for a moment.

So much for Phase 1. But Phase 2 also involves a certain degree of multi-tasking. If your notes are unclear or illegible, for example, your production will suffer because you will put too much effort into reading them. Clear notes, on the other hand, offer something akin to stage directions. Telling the interpreter when to pause, when to add emphasis and when not to.

If our mental capacity is finite, but we want to do more, then we have to learn to do some of the same tasks using less of our capacity on some or all of the tasks. How do we do this? Through automatization[§].

Automatization

Automatizing an activity means repeatedly using a consistent system for the completion of a task so that it requires less intellectual effort, (becomes automatic), thus leaving time and capacity for other tasks. In regard to learning automatization is also called internalization[§].

If a skill has been internalized, it requires less effort, less of your intellectual capacity to complete it. For example, if when speaking a foreign language you have to think about a particular grammar rule's correct application before you start speaking then you have not yet internalized that rule. If you speak fluently, which by definition means without stopping to think, then you have internalized all the rules. You correctly apply a consistent system without thinking about it. The thing about internalization, however, is that it **does not come from an intellectual understanding of how to complete a task but from repeated practice of the completion of the task**, until it is completed correctly WITHOUT thinking. To use the example of language again, you can tell someone that the third person singular conjugation of English verbs ends in -s, and pretty much everyone will understand this intellectually without any problem. Saying, *He offer me a drink*, however, is a very common mistake made by foreigners speaking English, even at advanced levels.

For trainee interpreters what this means is that I can tell you to note links[§]

in the margin[§] at the left of the page (Chapter 4), and you will understand me immediately, but it is not until you have practised doing it by noting dozens and dozens of different speeches that it will come so naturally that you don't have to think about it. And this is what is required if you are to free up intellectual resources for listening to the original. Note-taking is a mechanical activity; therefore it can be made automatic, internalized. Also, it is involved in both phases of consecutive interpreting to some degree, so any reduction in the effort required to take good notes will have a positive effect on both phases of your consecutive interpreting.

The application of a well practised and thought-out system will mean that the whole exercise of consecutive interpreting becomes less of an effort.

It follows also that internalization is easier if we take one thing at a time; consequently each of the component elements of the note-taking system proposed here is introduced one at a time, so that each can be internalized in turn. In this way each new chapter builds on the ideas of the previous one.

A bottom-up approach[§]

The interpreter working in consecutive mode listens to part of the source speech and instantaneously analyses what they have heard before taking notes. In this book we will see that we can reverse this order of things, and that learning a note-taking system can also be used as a means of highlighting methods for the analysis of source speeches.

This note-taking system is based on a number of characteristic and frequently occurring oratorical devices and structural elements in source speeches. By introducing them first as part of a note-taking system, these same elements and devices, of which you, the student interpreter, may not previously have been aware, are drawn to your attention. You can then identify them more easily when listening to source speeches, transfer them to your notepad and reproduce them in your interpretation.

In learning to use this note-taking system you will be practising the same analysis of source speeches that went into creating it. For example, if in Chapter 5 we say "note elements of equal value parallel on the page" you will start looking at the "value" of different elements of the speech and how they compare to one another, which you may not have been doing before. You will be learning to analyse the source text[§].

Learning by doing

> Tell me and I will forget,
> Show me and I will remember,
> Involve me and I will understand.

This is the ancient Chinese motto by which many teachers, particularly in the

Teaching English as a Foreign Language and corporate training sectors are trained. They are the words of the student to their teacher and they mean that we learn best how to complete a task not by understanding intellectually how it is done (because we have been told how), but by actually completing the task ourselves – perhaps with some non-intrusive guidance from the teacher. "Learning by doing" has long been the mantra of interpreter trainers, although books on interpreting have found it difficult to do other than "tell" readers about interpreting. This book seeks to "show" the reader clear examples of the skills described and "involve" the reader by asking them to think for themselves and to come up with their own answers by completing a number of tasks set. The versions given at the back of the book for the same tasks are no more than suggestions. They are not "right". There is no "right" way to do things, but some are better than others!

About the notes

This note-taking system has its roots in the Indo-European languages of Europe. For example it reads from left to right and is built around the word order of these languages. There are historical and practical reasons for this: conference interpreting was born in Europe and much of its literature written there; also this author has only limited experience of languages outside the Indo-European family. Nonetheless, much of the system can still apply and, in theory, can be adjusted to suit other types of languages: for example it can be written from right to left so that it reads from right to left. The principles will still apply, the practice is left to you.

This note-taking system is not the creation of any one interpreter, even if some had a bigger hand in it than others. It is a compilation of the best of many interpreters' ideas taken from detailed reading of much of the available literature (see bibliography); from working with other interpreters and discussing their notes with them; from my own experience as a trainer (and, once upon a time, as a student!) and from a knowledge of the problems that student interpreters most commonly encounter. I have compiled solutions and presented this collection of ideas for note-taking in what I hope is a methodical and clear manner. The novelty, if there is one, is that these ideas are presented together and in a way that allows you to progress step-by-step towards the acquisition of a sound note-taking system.

By the time you have worked your way through this book you will be able to take notes that are clear, consistent and efficient; notes which back up your memory when it needs help and let it do its work when it doesn't. It is a system which will help you to analyse the incoming source speech, because to use the system you will have to have thought about the original BEFORE you write anything down.

The system will not necessarily arm you for every eventuality, but it will prepare you for most of them. It is not everything you need to know about note-taking, but a lot of it. Remember your notes are only one of several skills that make up consecutive interpreting! This note-taking system is a flexible basis on which you will build your own ideas. And I would be very surprised, even disappointed, if most readers did not introduce a considerable number of their own ideas into their own notes.

It has been said that note-taking cannot be taught, and that everyone must come up with their own system. This is quite wrong. While no two interpreters will ever produce an identical set of notes, most speeches present the interpreter with a limited range of the same problems, for which effective solutions have already been worked out and are applied by many, many interpreters. These techniques are described in this book, as are ways of practising and internalizing their use. The book, then, offers you a sound basic system for note-taking in consecutive interpreting. You can add to it, customize it, ignore bits of it to your heart's content, but the idea is that it will stop you trying to reinvent what is already there.

About the examples

The examples in this book are all real speeches given by English native-speakers and which are available on the Internet. The first time each speech is used as an example you will find a brief explanation of where, when, why and to whom the speaker was speaking. A list of these speeches, speakers and Internet addresses can be found in Part III, The Back of the Book (page 226). You will also find there a number of Internet addresses where you can find speeches in other languages.

I have used the same speeches to demonstrate ideas from several chapters in this book, not because I was too lazy to go out and find a new speech for each example, but to show that all the elements of discourse described in this book, and for which a technique for note-taking in consecutive is suggested, are to be found in almost any speech. It is precisely because they recur so frequently that it is possible and desirable to have ready technique for their notation.

This book, and all the notes in it, are monolingual, meaning that notes from English texts are taken in English. One reason for this is that monolingual note-taking from source speeches in your mother tongue[§] to notes in your mother tongue will be our point of departure. However, more important is that being monolingual the book is accessible to the widest number of people. Had I used French texts with English notes and commentary, only the limited number of people with BOTH these languages in their combination would have been able to fully benefit from the book.

How to use the book

Recommended progression for Part I

It is recommended that you first try the exercises in each chapter using written texts[§] of speeches in your mother tongue. By "written texts" I mean the verbatim transcript of a speech that a speaker has given orally in public. Tips on where to find such material are given below. When you are comfortable completing the exercises assigned and have attained some proficiency in each technique, you should move on to transcripts of foreign-language speeches. These exercises are done from PAPER TO PAPER: you will transform the written text into written notes as described in the exercise you are doing. Do not read the written word out loud. Work with the spoken word comes later, and as we will see in the section Moving On…, we will NOT be reading out speeches verbatim from texts to do this. If your mother tongue is not English you should look for examples from your own language to work with. You will find some pointers on where to find such material below and at the back of the book. When you have completed Chapters 1-4 using written texts as sources, read the section Moving On… and then return to Chapter 1 and repeat the same exercises from the spoken word.

Why do I suggest working from transcripts first, rather than from the spoken word? Taking notes and listening at the same time is too much to do for any new interpreter. It has been too much for everyone who has ever started learning consecutive interpreting. It only becomes "not too much" when some tasks have become internalized with experience and practice. By practising note-taking from the written word you will learn the techniques of note-taking without the time pressure or multi-tasking that is involved when we have to listen to a speech and take notes at the same time. Starting with texts gives us all the time we need to familiarize ourselves with and practise the new techniques of note-taking, so that when we start doing the same from the spoken word the note-taking itself is less of a novelty. This means that intellectual capacity is freed up and can be devoted to listening. The fact that taking notes from a written text is a slightly artificial exercise (in that you will never to do it professionally) is in my view, and my experience, far outweighed by the benefits explained here and later in the section Moving On...

Chapters 1 and 2 are devoted entirely to work on recognizing and breaking down some of the most commonly occurring structures in the type of public discourse most commonly interpreted in consecutive mode. Actual note-taking only begins in Chapter 3, and then initially from written texts, not the spoken word. There is no reproduction of source speeches (no production phase[§]) until after Chapter 4. This may frustrate those who want to do everything right from the word "Go!", but a establishing a sound basis will be worth a little frustration.

In fact progress will not be that slow. If you spend just one week on each chapter you will have completed Chapters 1- 4 once each with the written and then spoken word in eight weeks. That is just one third of the shortest available postgraduate interpreting courses, so you see, there is really no need to rush. You will still have two thirds of the year to practise, but with the advantage that, having mastered a sound technique for note-taking it will no longer cause you problems. You will be able to concentrate on production, style, reformulation, etc. Remember, though, when we say one week per chapter that doesn't mean reading a chapter, putting the book down, doing nothing for a week and then coming back to look at the next chapter. It means working and practising regularly and frequently on the basis of what is described in a chapter for a week, and then moving on.

Below is a suggestion as to how you might work through the book. Start by working through the chapters with written source texts.

Week		Source	
1	Chapter 1	written texts in mother tongue	no production phase from notes taken
2	Chapter 1	written texts in foreign language	no production phase from notes taken
3	Chapter 2	written texts in mother tongue	no production phase from notes taken
4	Chapter 2	written texts in foreign language	no production phase from notes taken
5	Chapter 3	written texts in mother tongue	no production phase from notes taken
6	Chapter 3	written texts in foreign language	no production phase from notes taken
7	Chapter 4	written texts in mother tongue	begin reproducing speeches in mother tongue from notes (from mother-tongue source)
8	Chapter 4	written texts in foreign language	begin reproducing speeches in your mother tongue from notes (from a foreign language source speech)

Then move on to the spoken word. When working with the spoken word follow the guidelines in the section Moving On… The source speeches for ALL your practice should be given by your colleagues from the notes taken in Week 8 above and subsequently.

Week		Source	
9	Chapter 1	spoken speeches in mother tongue	no production phase from notes taken
	Chapter 1	spoken speeches in foreign language	no production phase from notes taken
	(Chapter 2 is for work with written word only so we skip it here)		
10	Chapter 3	spoken speeches in mother tongue	no production phase from notes taken
11	Chapter 3	spoken speeches in foreign language	no production phase from notes taken
13	Chapter 4	spoken speeches in mother tongue	Begin reproducing speeches in mother tongue from notes (from mother-tongue source)
14	Chapter 4	spoken speeches in foreign language	Begin reproducing speeches in mother tongue from notes (from L2 source)

At this stage you will have the basics of a sound system for note-taking and it is worth pausing a while to practise what you already know for a few weeks.

When you're ready to continue the pattern suggested here for Chapter 5 can also be used for the remaining chapters.

Week		Source	
15	Chapter 5	written texts in mother tongue	1. no production phase from notes taken
			2. add production phase when comfortable with ideas
16	Chapter 5	written texts in foreign language	production phase
17	Chapter 5	spoken speeches in mother tongue	1. no production phase from notes taken
			2. add production phase when comfortable with ideas
18	Chapter 5	spoken speeches in foreign language	production phase

The progression described above is no more than a guideline. You could equally go through the book from start to finish working mother tongue to mother tongue, and then return to the beginning to work through again from a foreign language into your mother tongue. What is important is that you do it step-by-step. Understanding the ideas in this book is no great intellectual feat, but understanding them is not the same as being able to use and apply them without thinking. To do that you will have to practise – a lot.

Parts II-III

As explained above, Part II is not an integral part of the progression outlined in Part I but a complement to it. Part III contains a series of example notes with commentary along with versions of the tasks set in the different chapters and a variety of additional information that may be of use.

Further exercises

At the risk of repeating myself, practice is an essential part of learning to become an interpreter, and the same applies to learning to take notes in consecutive interpreting. Repeating chapters, practising regularly with colleagues and alone several times a week, if not every day, is the only way to internalize these techniques so that they become a reflex.

Where to find practice material

More practice exercises for consecutive interpreting (as well as for language acquisition and simultaneous interpreting) can be found in Gillies (2004). Where to find material to practise note-taking with is explained below.

The type of speech you should use for the exercises in this book and for your own further practice can be found very easily on the Internet. Ministers are often out and about, speaking in situations that mirror those in which consecutive interpreting is used, and most ministries, certainly the major ones like Foreign Affairs, archive their ministers' speeches and make them available on their websites. Look out for ministers speaking abroad, where they may really have been interpreted and don't be afraid of junior ministers. They often speak to smaller gatherings and are even more likely to be suitable for consecutive. Ambassadors' speeches can also be useful, and, because by definition they tend to be speaking abroad, you may well find speeches that were actually interpreted consecutively at the time. Remember, also, that for many of you (who work with English, German, French, Portuguese or Spanish for example), speeches given by the ministers of other countries which have the same official language can also be used as practice material. This will help you acquire a broader knowledge of your languages, improve your general knowledge AND give you a huge source of practice material.

Big companies and charities, as well as NGOs and international institutions are also places to look for ceremonial speeches, speeches of introduction or inauguration. These are among the types of speeches you want to be looking for, that is, speeches that could have been interpreted consecutively. Don't use newspaper articles as they do not properly reflect the conventions of the spoken word. And don't use the written word as you find it on websites.

Unfortunately most of the speeches that are actually interpreted consecutively don't make it onto the Internet, so when looking for practice material we should try to find speeches that could have been given in the same sort of situation as where consecutive is used, or which are similar in tone and content to such speeches. I have outlined above the type of speeches that are most commonly interpreted consecutively.

This means that you should also beware of speeches given in national parliaments without ruling them out completely. Parliaments' websites offer a ready source of material for the exercises in this book, and some examples of such speeches can be found in this book. But many speeches are much more dense than those interpreted consecutively and are not suitable, particularly at this early stage in your training. If you are going to use speeches from parliamentary debates try to stick to formal addresses on special occasions or introductory remarks in a debate. In real life, of course, speeches in national parliaments are not interpreted consecutively. At the back of the book you will find more ideas about where to find practice material (page 230).

The way this material can best be used and the advantages of doing so are explained in the section Moving On....

Miscellaneous

Equipment

Interpreters working in consecutive mode generally use notepads to take notes on, although sheets of paper and, in extremis, napkins and menus have been known to be requisitioned. For the sake of your nerves, though, it is best to be well prepared and have a notepad and pen with you at all times, particularly if the organizer of your meeting (or teacher) says, "No, there won't be any consecutive"! Different interpreters also favour different types of pad, paper and writing utensil. You can try them all out, but the vast majority of colleagues use the following for the reasons explained alongside.

Reporter's notepad	10 x 15 cm*	A convenient size. Big enough for clear notes, small enough to carry around.
	Spiral bound from the top	Pages turn easily and never get lost, dropped or mixed up.
	Firm sheet of card as the back page	You will often have to take notes and speak standing up. Try doing either of these with a floppy notepad!

	Plain pages, or with lines or squares as feint as possible	What you write must be clearly visible on the paper you are using.
	Write on one side of the page only.	The order of the pages gets very confusing if you don't.
Biro	Writes quickly, smoothly, clearly and quietly.	Some interpreters use pencils but fountain pens, felt tips and rollerballs are a No-No. They are slow to write with, and prone to running out and smudging.
	Several spares	If it can run out it will. Bring a spare, or two!
	The ink must be clearly visible on the paper you are using.	

*If you often work standing up, you may prefer an A4 pad, as this can be held against the body more easily for support. A pad smaller than 10 x 15 cm might be easy to carry round with you unobtrusively in a pocket. There are pros and cons with both.

What language to note in

Opinions differ on this question but all the techniques described in this book can be used regardless of what language you note in. For more views on the subject have a look at some of the books in the bibliography where a variety of opinions are expressed, all the way from "note in the source language§" to "note in the target language§"! In the end it will come down to which language you feel more comfortable with, and that often means noting predominantly in your mother tongue regardless of whether it is the source or target language. For a fuller discussion of this point, see Van Dam (2004).

Reading back notes

It seems most sensible to talk about reading back from your notes after you have worked through at least part of this book rather than before, so here I will confine myself to mentioning that there is no better description of the technique interpreters should use to read back from their notes when interpreting consecutively than that given by Roderick Jones (2002:64). You can find it in the section Moving On…, (page 72).

Chapter 1 Speech Analysis

In Chapters 1, 2 and 3 there will be no actual interpreting, or rather there will be no production phase. You will not be giving an oral presentation of your version of the source texts. We will not try to reproduce speeches until we have the basic elements of a note-taking system that will allow us to do this usefully.

Before we start looking at how to take notes, let us spend a little time looking at the mechanics of the speeches that we will be listening to, taking notes from and, later, interpreting. Throughout your work as an interpreter you will listen to speeches in a quite different way to the ordinary listener. You will not only be listening to the words and the content as the normal listener does, but you will also be dissecting the speech in your head, analysing its structure and progression to find out what fits with what and why. You will identify the communicative function of different parts of the speech; you will recognize the main ideas and the secondary ones; you will spot the links between them; and more besides.

To give you an idea of how this can be done, this chapter offers a number exercises in which we will look at speeches at a "macro-" level; that is, we will not worry about the words or the content so much but rather we will look at the framework of the speech. This framework, the skeleton of a speech, is of great interest to the interpreter, because without it, the flesh, the details, have nothing to hang on and are meaningless.

Speech writing guides

Many speeches that you will have to interpret consecutively will be ceremonial, they will be speeches of welcome, inaugurations, or after dinner speeches. You should be aware that speakers, even if improvising, will often stick to certain conventions. Some speakers are naturals, some have speeches written for them, others learn how to speak from guide books and manuals (and some, who perhaps should, unfortunately don't!).

You don't need to re-invent the wheel and start learning to analyse speeches from scratch. There is a good chance that much of any given speech adheres to standard conventions for speeches of the same type. You can call on the expertise of speech writers, and speaking trainers to help you recognize these conventions. This will give you a head start in learning to analyse speeches for yourself and help to recognize the component parts of speeches you are listening to by giving you an X-ray picture of the speech itself.

Books on "Giving good speeches" can be found very easily in bookshops or on the Internet and they can be very useful. Another very good source of tips on giving good speeches, are the toastmasters' websites around the globe. Toastmasters speak for a living and they generally know their stuff. Let's take one example from the many books on the market. In his book *Writing Great Speeches*, Alan Perlman (1998:69-80) suggests the following guidelines for public speakers introducing other speakers. This type of speech is very common at meetings and events where consecutive is used, although of course it is not the only type of speech you will have to interpret consecutively. His pointers are summarized in the table below.

Speeches of introduction

Aim of the speech is to:

1. give a sense of what is to come
2. familiarize the audience with the speaker's achievements
   e.g. biographical details / anecdotes / items of specific relevance to this audience
3. create a sense of anticipation

Structure should:

4. add finesse to the obvious. If the audience are already familiar with the biographical details of the person being introduced add phrases like, "as we all know...", "you'll all be familiar with..."
5. be maximum 7 minutes in length
6. be positive always
7. build suspense

Speech will include:

8. quotes
9. link to theme of today's conference
10. characteristic of speaker to follow plus illustration of same
11. applause markers e.g. "please join me in welcoming..."(These are numbers assigned for the purposes of this exercise not by Perlman.)

For the interpreter working in consecutive mode, knowing in advance that this sort of thinking goes into the preparation of the speech we will have to interpret is very useful. Speeches are not plucked from thin air, they have an underlying structure holding them together. Naturally good speakers do this without thinking about it; conscientious speakers read books like Perlman's; bad speakers do neither but we have to interpret them anyway and the interpreter may improve on the original.

Even the apparently very obvious pointers should be interesting here as they come from a professional speaker, rather than an interpreter AND are very relevant for the interpreter trying to anticipate and prepare for such a job. Just from the above list interpreters have many clues about what to expect and how to speak themselves. Biographical details; length of speech; mood; building to a climax; the end will be important; watch out for quotations; background on today's meeting; dramatic pauses required in interpreting as well as original: having familiarized yourself with these guidelines you are less likely to be surprised by what the speaker says.

Speeches of introduction are not, of course, the only type of speech that is interpreted consecutively. Also you should be aware that conventions for public speakers may differ from country to country. Look also at similar guides in all the languages you interpret from and into.

Example

The following is a speech by Michael H. Moskow, President of the Federal Reserve Bank of Chicago, given to the 39th Annual Conference on Bank Structure and Competition, at the Fairmont Hotel in Chicago on May 8th 2003. In it Mr Moskow introduces Alan Greenspan, Chairman of the Federal Reserve System, the US Central Bank, as guest speaker to the assembled bankers. Mr Greenspan will speak via video-link. The conference deals with the subject of corporate governance and takes place amid a number of scandals highlighting the failure of the same in the U.S. Mr Moskow refers to this in his introduction. Henceforth references to this speech will be to **Moskow**. For the full text of the speech see the URL given at the back of the book (page 226).

Where, in this speech, examples of the techniques recommended on the previous page occur I have marked them with the appropriate number from the box above. So [3] refers to "creating a sense of anticipation". See if you agree with my suggestions.

> It's my great pleasure to welcome you to our 39th annual conference on bank structure and competition. This year's focus on corporate governance[1][9] is especially relevant.
>
> We've seen too many once-revered companies end up severely damaged, in some cases beyond repair, by failures in corporate governance. Arthur Andersen, Enron, Global Crossing, HealthSouth, Quest, Tyco, WorldCom...the list goes on, and the headlines continue to appear, even today [9]. Deficiencies include inadequate board oversight, misleading or even fraudulent accounting practices, questionable audit arrangements and efforts to hide the truth. Thousands of jobs and billions of dollars of shareholder value have been lost. And we've seen the spectacle of corporate executives being led away in handcuffs[3].
>
> Those of you in financial firms are affected through your credit exposure to firms that followed questionable accounting practices, and through your own corporate governance practices. This has led to greater investor skepticism and increased uncertainty in the equity and credit markets. And uncertainty affects asset prices and can negatively impact the economy[3].

During the conference you'll be discussing these issues in greater detail[1].

The role of boards of directors. Changes in financial regulation, accounting standards and disclosure rules. The impact on financial firms and financial markets[1].

In this effort, we have enlisted some of the most prominent members of the financial industry to speak with you this week[9]. They include banking executives, regulatory authorities, administration officials and financial and legal scholars[1].

Perhaps the most eagerly awaited speaker in this stellar line-up, however, is the person I'm about to introduce- a man, really, who needs no introduction[3 4]. We have the privilege of hearing from someone whose accomplishments and stature have made him a respected name throughout the world[3]. Someone whose words are analyzed by everyone from Wall Street to Main Street[2]. And someone whose unquestioned integrity[4] stands out even more brightly today, at a time when negative behavior seems to be darkening the news[3 4 9].

He is Alan Greenspan, chairman of the board of governors of the Federal Reserve System[2]. Alan, we wish you could be here in person, as you have been every year since the conference began. But we know you've been advised, after minor surgery, to stay put for a while[6].

Alan Greenspan is serving his fourth four-year term as chairman[2], having been designated to this position by Presidents Reagan, Bush Senior and Clinton. It was in August 1987 when he originally took office as chairman and to fill an unexpired term on the Board[2]. He also serves as chairman of the Federal Open Market Committee[2], the System's principal monetary policymaking body.

Most important, as I'm sure you're all aware [9], the current President Bush thinks "Alan Greenspan should get another term," and the chairman has said he'll serve if nominated. I think we'd all agree this is great news for our country and for the economy.

The details of Alan's background and his tremendous achievements are well documented[4]. His bachelors, masters and doctorate degrees in economics from New York University[2]. His 30-year career as head of Townsend-Greenspan, an economic consulting firm in New York City[2]. And his service as chairman of the President's Council of Economic Advisers under President Ford[2], as well as on many other public and private boards[2].

He's received numerous awards and honors for his work, and his outstanding reputation and extraordinary talents are widely known[2]. Over the course of more than a decade, his adept handling of his complex responsibilities at the Fed have made him a hero - not only to people in business and government, but to millions of average citizens from all walks of life. It's truly a great honor to have the chairman as our keynote speaker[7].

Please join me in welcoming Alan Greenspan[11 5].

Additional comments

[3] All of the first paragraphs create a certain sense of anticipation.....how is all this relevant to today?.....well we're going to talk about it.
[6] general mood is clearly positive, if not showman-like!

Not all of the elements from the list on page 18 are included, of course, but you can see that many of the elements of our "guide" do appear, although this speaker has probably never read Perlman's book, he is sticking to many of the conventions which Perlman describes, having listened to hundreds of similar speeches. You will find that many good speaking guides offer similar advice.

Exercise

Try to do the same with the speech below. Compare the results with colleagues.

These remarks were made by the president of the organization Computer Professionals for Corporate Responsibility (CPSR), Terry Winograd, upon presentation of the first Norbert Wiener Award for Social and Professional Responsibility. Norbert Wiener is held by CPSR to have laid the foundations for many aspects of modern computing, as well as being a leader in assessing the social implications of that new and emerging technology. For this reason a prize in his name is awarded by CPSR for outstanding contributions in the field of Corporate Social Responsibility. Norbert Wiener died in 1964. The award is made to Professor David Lorge Parnas. The speech is made after a dinner, held for several hundred people. Henceforth references to this speech will be to **Winograd**. For the full text of the speech see the URL given at the back of the book (page 226).

> Tonight we begin a new tradition for CPSR, presenting for the first time the Norbert Wiener Award for Social and Professional Responsibility. It is especially fitting that we initiate it here at MIT*, which was the intellectual home to Norbert Wiener for more than forty years.....
>
> So we might think of Norbert Wiener as the patron saint of CPSR, although I suspect he would be a bit uncomfortable with the religious metaphor.
>
> Tonight we are honoring a man who, like Wiener, might not fit the model of sainthood but who, like Wiener, has served as a visible and inspiring example of social responsibility: David Lorge Parnas.
>
> David Parnas is Professor of Computer Science and Queen's University in Kingston, Ontario. He received Bachelors, Masters, and Ph.D. degrees from the Carnegie Institute of Technology (now Carnegie Mellon University) and has taught at a number of prominent institutions in the United States, Germany, and Canada. His research has been extremely influential in the field of software engineering, of which he can rightfully be called a founder. He was one of the pioneers in work on structured programming, and his research still stands as a classic in that area.
>
> On the basis of his work on making programming more productive and reliable, he was made head of the Software Engineering Research Section and director of the project on Software Cost Reduction at the Naval Research Laboratory, beginning in 1979. His expertise made him a natural choice to serve on the panel formed in 1985 to investigate the feasibility of the computing system required for the Strategic Defense Initiative ("Star Wars") program proposed by President Reagan.
>
> I do not need to rehearse for this group the subsequent story (which Professor Parnas elaborated in this remarks on the panel discussion on ethics). To summarize quickly, he attended one meeting of the panel (now known as the Eastport Group) and recognized that the project was ill-conceived and

unworkable.

He raised his concerns with his colleagues on the panel, and although they could not refute his arguments, they saw the program as an opportunity to develop expanded research funding for computer science and did not want to hinder that bonanza (in which their own institutions would obviously share). After trying to take his concerns to the relevant government officials and failing to get their cooperation, he went public with a carefully written and cogent series of articles (later published in the Communications of the ACM** and American Scientist) which still stand as the basic argument against the feasibility of SDI***.

*   Massachussets Institute of Technology. A very well-known and prestigious US University.

**   Association for Computing Machinery. Its *Communications* is a scientific magazine covering computing issues.

***   Strategic Defense Initiative. Missile defence system proposed by Ronald Reagan. Also known as Star Wars.

Compare with the version at the back of the book (p209).

How to practise - speaking guides

First of all you will practise with the transcripts of speeches.

1. Download the texts of speeches of introduction from the Internet and see if you can identify any of the points that are listed above (Perlman's list) in the same way as you have done in this chapter.

2. If your mother tongue is not English, find a guide like the one above in your own language and draw up a summary list of main pointers for speeches of introduction.

3. Find other guides to giving good speeches - what other types of speeches are there and what do these books recommend speakers include in them? Make a list, download speeches for each type from the Internet and see if you can identify any of the points in those speeches. Do this first with books and speeches in your mother tongue.

> In *Conference Interpreting Explained* Jones (2002:14-21) describes four basic types of speech: logical argument "for" and "against"; logical one-sided argument leading to some conclusion; a narrative speech; a descriptive speech.
> When reading or listening to speeches see which of these categories your source speech falls into, and before you do anything with a speech try to identify it as one of these.

4. Now find similar guides in the foreign languages you work from. Make a

summary list of the main points of advice to speakers. Download examples of the type of speech described, in the same language as the guide and work through them in the same way as above, comparing the actual speech with the guide's advice. Make a note of the different conventions between languages.

5. Compare your work regularly with colleagues and ask teachers for input as well.

Justifying and explaining your decisions to others, or failing to, is an excellent way of learning. Remember though, there are no right answers, the only right answer is the one that works for you.

6. Try to write your own speeches using the guidelines above (Perlman) and those you have discovered when looking at other guides (Point 2 in this section).

Later you can do the same from spoken speeches given by fellow students or using the speeches you have written in Point 6 (and following the guidelines in the section Moving On…). Try to avoid reading texts out verbatim.

7. You won't have time to note everything down when listening to a spoken speech. So, using the guidelines for good speeches that you have read, make yourself a table like the one below to practise with. Each time you recognize one of the recommended elements of a speech tick a box next to it in the table or if you have time note a word that will remind you of it.

…sense of what is to come	*Eagerly awaited*	√			
…speaker's achievements	√	*chairman of*			
…create a sense of anticipation	√	√			
…add finesse to the obvious					
Etc.					

8. Do the same with different types of speeches, first in your mother tongue and then later in your other languages.

Structure maps[§]

Another way of looking at the macro-elements of a speech is to create structure maps. That is to summarize not the content of the speech, but the function and structure of its component parts alongside the original text. Look at the examples below.

Example 1

Speech given by Tony Blair, Prime Minister of the UK, on measures to combat anti-social behaviour. Mr Blair is speaking on 14th October at Queen Elizabeth II Conference Centre, London, to an audience of police officers from around the country. Its topic is the introduction of new legal measures to curb anti-social behaviour, particularly in young people, an issue that has been given a lot of press coverage in the months prior to the speech. Henceforth references to this speech will be to **Blair 1**. For the full text of the speech see the URL given at the back of the book on page 226.

I want to make one very simple point in this speech. To the police, housing officers, local authorities - we've listened, we've given you the powers, and it's time to use them.	*What is he going to say and to whom?*
You've got new powers to deal with nuisance neighbours - use them.	*Example of "What". 1*
You've got new powers to deal with abandoned cars - use them.	*"What". 2*
You've got new powers to give fixed penalty fines for anti-social behaviour - without going through a long court process, use them.	*"What". 3*
The new legislation, the ASB* Unit in the Home Office, this Action Plan we launched today has been two years in the making. In this time, I have visited many estates and talked to local people about their concerns. Two things emerged. First, ASB is for many the number one item of concern right on their doorstep - the graffiti, vandalism, dumped cars, drug dealers in the street, abuse from truanting school-age children. Secondly, though many of these things are in law a criminal offence, it is next to impossible for the police to prosecute without protracted court process, bureaucracy and hassle, when conviction will only result in a minor sentence.	*background* *2 points : point 1* *point 2*

Hence these new powers to take swift, summary action. The FPNs** were piloted in four local areas. Over 6000 fines were issued. The only complaint of the police was that the powers weren't wide enough. So we have listened, we have extended the powers, extended who can use them, and made them from early next year when the Bill becomes law, nation-wide.	*Therefore...* *...conclusions from the above.*

*   Anti-social behaviour

**   Fixed Penalty Notice. On-the-spot fine incurred for minor criminal offences. Designed to reduce bad behaviour on the streets and relieve some of the burden on the courts.

A breakdown doesn't have to look like this and there is no one right way to do this. What is important is that you start taking apart speeches in your head: that you try to identify what the speaker is trying to achieve with each part of what they are saying. A speech is not just a stream of words. It is a collection of ideas, which can be noted more easily and effectively if we first look at how they fit together.

Example 2

In this speech (henceforth **Buzek**), the then Polish Prime Minister, Jerzy Buzek, introduces a debate on European integration. The debate takes place against the backdrop of Poland's accession negotiations which must be concluded speedily if Poland is to join the EU as planned. (At this time that date was still 1st January 2003). The speech was given in the Polish Parliament, the Sejm, in the first quarter of 2000. As I have said above, this type of speech given in a national Parliament would rarely be interpreted in consecutive mode in real life, but for the purposes of the exercises in this chapter such speeches may be suitable, as in this example. The full original speech in Polish is available at the URL given at the back of the book (page 227).

Mr Speaker! Ladies and Gentlemen of the House! The subject of today's debate, Poland's integration with the European Union, should and will be the most important political topic of the next 12 and more months. This is clear from: the timetable for the current negotiations; the urgent tasks of introducing and implementing legislation and of exploiting assistance funds, but above all from the setting of 1st January 2003 as the date for Poland's entry into the European Union	*What are we talking about?* *Why? (list of 3)*

It has been almost six months since this House debated European integration in September. Since then there have been a number of significant events that may affect our path to the European Union, for example the Summit in Helsinki. Work was undertaken to adapt to the demands of Union membership; negotiations continued; discussions were held between the subsequent Presidencies of the Union, Finland and Portugal, the Foreign Minister and myself personally. We also sought to further our cause through diplomatic channels. It is time therefore that we in this House took stock of how far down the road to the European Union we are and where we go from here as a continuation of the debate on Europe begun here in September, a debate on the return of Europe to Poland and Poland to Europe.	*Events preceding this debate.....* *(list of 5)* *We conclude from this that we must....*

Exercise

Now try the same with the speech below.

In the following speech (henceforth **Torry 1**) British Ambassador to Germany, Sir Peter Torry, is speaking on 20ᵗʰ January 2004 at a function of the British Chamber of Commerce in Germany, at Duesseldorf Industrie Club. He had been in his post 6 months at the time and was speaking to an audience of around 300 business people, some of whom had the opportunity to put questions afterwards.

Ladies and Gentlemen,
    Many thanks for inviting me here this evening.
    I have been asked to talk about "Germany and Britain: Meeting the Economic Challenge Together".
    I think the "together" important. There is a great deal that we could do together and that we can learn from each other.
    As you would expect, I shall paint a positive picture. But there is one aspect which causes some concern.
    To be provocative - I fear that Britain and Germany have somehow drifted apart.	

Not so much at government level, where quite the contrary has happened, as I'll explain in a minute. But at a personal level. Twenty years ago, German was a major language in British schools and many school children would visit Germany on regular exchanges. Spanish has now overtaken German, and young people in Britain have less exposure to Germany as a result. The British Army Of the Rhine was in those days some 65,000 strong. If you include families, relatives etc, that gave many more thousand British people reason to visit Germany. The army is now around 20,000: so again a fall off. This ties in with another persistent element in our bilateral relationship: the image of Germany in Britain. I was looking recently at a survey of young people's attitudes in both countries. Germans see the UK as a good place to work and to study - second only to the US. They recognise that we have a creative, multicultural society. But Germans see us as reluctant Europeans. They have the impression that we don't like them very much. Young British people said they admired Germany's high-quality cars and its well-organised people. But they still associated Germany with the 12 years between 1933 and 1945. They thought Germans lacked a sense of humour and - astoundingly, since we always seem to lose to Germany - that they played bad football.	

Now compare your version with your colleagues' and the version at the back[§] of the book (page 210). Remember, the version at the back is not the "right" version; it is a version.

Mini-summaries[§]

A similar exercise would be to note a very brief summary of the main ideas in the right hand column rather than the structure as above. Look at the example below.

Example - Blair 1

I want to make one very simple point in this speech. To the police, housing officers, local authorities - we've listened, we've given you the powers, and it's time to use them.	*Use your new powers on.....*
You've got new powers to deal with nuisance neighbours - use them.	*nuisance neighbours*
You've got new powers to deal with abandoned cars - use them.	*cars*
You've got new powers to give fixed penalty fines for anti-social behaviour - without going through a long court process, use them.	*Anti-Social Behaviour (ASB)*
The new legislation, the ASB Unit in the Home Office, this Action Plan we launched today has been two years in the making. In this time, I have visited many estates and talked to local people about their concerns. Two things emerged. First, ASB is for many the number one item of concern right on their doorstep - the graffiti, vandalism, dumped cars, drug dealers in the street, abuse from truanting school-age children. Secondly, though many of these things are in law a criminal offence, it is next to impossible for the police to prosecute without protracted court process, bureaucracy and hassle, when conviction will only result in a minor sentence.	*people are concerned about* *1 ASB* *2 bureaucracy*
Hence these new powers to take swift, summary action. The FPNs were piloted in four local areas. Over 6000 fines were issued. The only complaint of the police was that the powers weren't wide enough. So we have listened, we have extended the powers, extended who can use them, and made them from early next year when the Bill becomes law, nation-wide.	*Therefore...new powers, which were a success in trials and have been extended.*

Exercise

Try the same on the speech below.

This speech (henceforth **Hodgson**)was delivered by New Zealand government Minister Pete Hodgson on 19th February 2004 to an audience of New Zealand dairy farmers at the Dairy Expo 2004, in the TSB Stadium, New Plymouth, New Zealand. The title of the speech was, "Why climate change matters". Although global warming may not affect New Zealand as much as other countries, New Zealand has been hit by damage to the ozone layer, so the public is sensitive to climate issues. Also this audience of farmers will have a vested interest in any, even minor changes to the climate. The full speech is available at the URL given at the back of the book on page 227.

For those of you who don't know me, I'm the Minister of Energy, Science, Fisheries and a few other things including climate change policy. It's that last one that has taken me up close and personal with dairy farmers and brought me the invitation to speak here today. So let's talk about the weather. I'm not about to tell you that the storms we're going through now are the result of climate change. I'm not a climatologist and I don't think even a climatologist would offer any conclusions on that score. But what I will tell you – and what a climatologist would tell you – is that this is what climate change looks like. One of the significant consequences expected from climate change is an increase in the frequency and severity of extreme weather events. This is why we use the term climate change in preference to global warming, because it more accurately captures the range of climatic effects that the enhanced greenhouse effect is expected to produce.	

A long-term increase in global average temperatures is the key indicator and consequence of the build-up of greenhouse gases in the Earth's atmosphere. But the expected effects of that change on the world's climate systems are multiple and diverse. The New Zealand dairy industry is founded on the superb conditions this country's climate provides for growing grass. This is why climate change matters to dairy farmers and – because of the economic importance of your industry – to New Zealand. We know climate change is already under way on a global scale and there do appear to be some measurable effects emerging in New Zealand. A study done for the Ministry for the Environment said a southward shift in subtropical pasture species might be one indicator, along with an increased frequency of warmer winters in recent decades. It also suggested that a recorded halving of the planted area in kiwifruit in Northland over the six years to 2001 could be at least partly attributable to a warming climate, leading to reduced productivity	

Now compare your version with your colleagues' and the version at the back of the book (page 211).

How to practise – structure maps and mini-summaries

1. Download the transcripts of speeches from the Internet - ministry and official websites usually offer many speeches that could be suitable. For where and how to find speeches in the Internet see pages 14 and 130.

2. First use the transcripts of speeches in your own language and subsequently in your foreign languages.

3. Copy the speech into one column of a two column table as above.

4. Repeat the different tasks described in "Structure maps" and "Mini-summaries" above and compare your results with colleagues and/or ask your teacher for

advice.

5. Later, after you have worked through Chapters 1-4 and the section Moving On…, try to make mini-summaries from the spoken word. The source speeches for this will be given by your colleagues from their notes. How this is done is explained in the section Moving On… Use your notepad and divide each part of your summary with a horizontal line across the page.

6. Also for practice with spoken speeches: try the following exercise. Listen to a speech without taking notes. When the speech has been completed, make some notes that will help you to reproduce the speech. Give a consecutive rendering of the speech. (This exercise was first described by Weber,1989:166.)

Mind maps[§]

A mind map is a way of organizing information on a piece of paper. Usually it takes the form of an organic chart, sometimes multi-coloured, laid out on a large sheet of paper. Words and drawings are connected to one-another on the page in various ways; by lines, by their position on the page relative to one another, etc. This form of representing ideas taps into the way the mind associates and recalls information and can therefore be useful in helping us to organize and remember information.

Example

This example is taken from a book of exercises for student interpreters, *Interpreting: From Preparation to Performance* (Szabo, 2003:134).

> In the long term the idea is to develop a European high-speed railway network with Paris at its centre. A line to the north will reach Brussels, where it can branch out to the east to Cologne, or continue further north to Amsterdam and later even Hamburg. To the south-east the line through Lyon will enter Italy through Turin and reach through Rome and Naples right down to the toe of Italy. And in the south-west a link up with Spain via Barcelona and then to Madrid will make it possible to extend the network down.

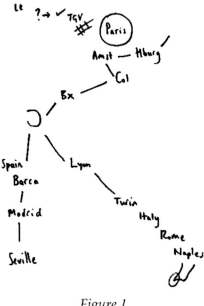

Figure 1

Exercise

Try the same with this speech in the box provided or on a pad of your own. Don't
worry if you can't get all of the ideas into your mind-map. That is not the point.
Just see how much of the speech you can note pictorially like this and whether
any or all of this structure would help you in reproducing the speech.

This speech (henceforth **Torry 2**) was given by Sir Peter Torry, British
Ambassador to Germany, in Hamburg, 24th July 2003, the 60th Anniversary of
the British bombing of Hamburg during the Second World War. He is speaking
to a predominantly German audience and tries to focus on the positive elements
linking Hamburg and the UK rather than on wartime events. As ambassador, one
of his jobs is to maintain good relations between the UK and Germany. The full
text of the speech is available at the URL given at the back of the book on page
227.

> Mr Mayor, Ladies and Gentlemen,
>
> Let me say first what a privilege it is for me, as British Ambassador in
> Germany, to have been invited by the City authorities to take part in this
> event.
>
> We are here today to remember a sombre and terrible moment in the
> recent history of Hamburg: the destruction of the City in July 1943 by the
> Royal Air Force.
>
> But this event today should also be about what has happened since those
> terrible days 60 years ago.
>
> The British attack on Hamburg was all the more tragic, since no other

German city has such strong links with Britain as Hamburg.

The relationship goes back many centuries. Indeed many of the peoples who settled in the British Isles in the 6th and 7th centuries came from around this area. If we could trace our ancestors' history back that far, we might find that the British are Hamburgers too.

In subsequent centuries the relationship between Britain and Hamburg grew through trading links such as the Guild of Merchant Adventurers established in 1611.

The first Anglican Church on the European continent was founded in Hamburg. British architects and engineers played a major role in the construction of the town in the 19th century.

Today more than 5,000 British people live in Hamburg. More tourists from Britain come to the city than from any other country.

And many of the big British companies have their German headquarters here: for example BAT or Unilever.

I think that this context of a shared history and a tradition of friendship is an important one to remember when we are remembering the events of the Second World War.

Three-dimensional mind maps

Often you will be called upon to interpret consecutively when travelling with a group. You may be visiting an industrial installation with a business delegation when the host decides to explain what everything is and does; or your group may be having a guided tour of a local tourist spot as part of their social and cultural programme; the possibilities are boundless. But what you will often find is that the machinery or building or whatever is being talked about by the speaker, and which is right in front of you to see and behold, can be used as a large three-dimensional mind map. You may not need to take notes at all if the speaker starts their explanation, say, at the top of the machine, building etc. and works their way down. The object, building, machine, landscape, whatever it might be, will be your notepad and mind map.

You can demonstrate this, and practise it, by preparing a large poster or a slide for an overhead projector depicting a building, a landscape, a machine or, in fact, whatever you like. Bring it into class, make sure your colleagues can see the poster/projection and now give an explanation of between two and four minutes of what can be seen. Nobody should take any notes while you are speaking. You will find that they will be able to reproduce a lot of the original speech if you leave the image where they can see it.

How to practise - mind maps

1. Download the transcripts of speeches from the Internet.

NB Not all speeches will lend themselves to this technique and some parts of a speech may be easier to work with than others. Don't worry! The idea is not to mind-map everything but to get into the habit of breaking down speeches in a variety of different ways.

2. First use speeches in your own language and subsequently in your foreign languages.

3. Repeat the task described above and compare your results with colleagues and/or ask your trainer for advice.

4. When you are comfortable with the technique, try to create mind maps from the spoken word as well. You may even find this easier than using the written word despite the increased time pressure.

Chapter 2   Recognizing and Splitting Ideas

The most oft repeated thing you will hear as a student interpreter is "note the ideas and not the words!". But what is an idea§? And how can we recognize them so that we can reproduce them properly in interpretation? You might say that a whole speech boils down to one idea, but will that help us in our note-taking? Each word might seem like an idea, but they won't all be as important as each other.

The first thing to understand is that when interpreters or your teachers say "the ideas and not the words" they are using the term "idea" to refer to two different things. For the purposes of this book and in order to be clear and consistent, I wish to keep them separate. First of all there are the "ideas" that we are going to deal with in this chapter, that is "parts of the message" (Thierry, 1981), those which tell us *who did what to whom"*. These "ideas" I am going to carry on calling "ideas".

Secondly there are "ideas" described by Rozan (1956), meaning the underlying meaning of a word or expression as being more important than the actual word(s) chosen to represent that meaning. For example the words *declare*, *say*, *tell* and *express*, can be considered synonymous: they have the same underlying meaning and would all be noted with the same symbol§ as a result. We will come to this a little later in the book. (See the end of Chapter 3, page 53, and Chapter 6, Symbols, page 99). These underlying meanings we are going to call "concepts§".

Question: What is an idea? This question is a little too metaphysical for this type of book, so let's come down to earth a bit...What is the basic unit for communicating something, anything in language? How do we say, *"Who does what to whom"*?

Answer: The sentence.

Question: And what are the basic units of a sentence?

Answer: The Subject, the Verb and often an Object of the verb (henceforth, SVO§).

Example

This is a speech (henceforth **Patten**) given by Chris Patten, then European Commissioner for External Relations, to the plenary session of the European Parliament on July 3rd 2000. He is reporting on the European Council of Ministers summit in Feira, Portugal, a few days earlier. In this extract he is speaking about relations with Russia.

> We took stock of the European Union's relations with Russia and the
> situation there, including in Chechnya, in the light of the recent EU-Russia
> Summit, which I think was regarded as fairly successful.

It is a long sentence, but what is the basic idea it conveys, the framework
on which the rest hangs? Ask yourself instead "*Who does what to whom (or to
what)*?". What is the basic Subject Verb Object make up of this sentence?

     S   V   O   O

     We .... took stock of.......   relations.... and the situation.

There are two objects, which sometimes happens, but you get the
picture.

We are going to bend the definitions used in describing language and
consider that the verbs "to be" and "there is/are" take Objects. This means then
that the expressions, *The report is interesting* and, *There is a rumour* are going to
be considered as Subject Verb Object units. Furthermore we will lump Direct and
Indirect Objects together under the heading of Object. Thus, *The Prime Minister
was speaking to an assembly of business leaders* will also be considered as SVO,
with *an assembly of business leaders* as the Object.

This rather relaxed approach to linguistic terminology may annoy
grammaticians and linguistics experts but, as you will see, it is going to make
note-taking much easier, and that is what we're here for. Let's look at another
example:

> In the areas for which I have some responsibility, there were also, as the
> Prime Minister has mentioned, some important developments at Feira.

Again it is a long sentence, but the basic idea, the SVO set up is very
simple.

there... were.... developments

Most of this sentence is additional information, the crux of what is being
said though, can be found in the SVO unit *there were developments.* If we miss
that, the rest of the sentence is meaningless. As you do more and more consecutive
interpreting you will see, and interpreters will tell you, that consecutive is really
about recognizing the core message in amongst all the other information. This is
how we start doing that.

For the purposes of note-taking in consecutive interpreting an idea is a...

SUBJECT - VERB - OBJECT group.

See how it works in the text below where we will look for these SVO units.

Step 1

To begin with, download the text of a speech into your word-processing software. Then we remove the paragraph spaces that were in the original to give us a block of text. The two versions of the example below show what this might look like.

Example

> In the areas for which I have some responsibility, there were also, as the Prime Minister has mentioned, some important developments at Feira. We took stock of the European Union's relations with Russia and the situation there, including in Chechnya, in the light of the recent EU-Russia Summit, which I think was regarded as fairly successful. It is too early to judge President Putin's economic programme; however, our basic message is that a sound programme will be vital to boost investor confidence.
>
> On Chechnya, there have, it is true, been some recent moderately positive developments in response to international and European Union pressure: for example the recent ECHO* mission was able to take place and western humanitarian agencies have greater access to the area. The conflict nevertheless continues and we still have considerable concerns. In particular, we want to see much greater access for humanitarian aid agencies. We want to see genuinely independent investigation into reports of human rights abuses, and we want to see a real dialogue between the Russian government and the Chechens.

* The Humanitarian Aid Office of the European Union.

The text above is transformed into the block of text below.

> In the areas for which I have some responsibility, there were also, as the Prime Minister has mentioned, some important developments at Feira. We took stock of the European Union's relations with Russia and the situation there, including in Chechnya, in the light of the recent EU-Russia Summit, which I think was regarded as fairly successful. It is too early to judge President Putin's economic programme; however, our basic message is that a sound programme will be vital to boost investor confidence. On Chechnya, there have, it is true, been some recent moderately positive developments in response to international and European Union pressure: for example the recent

ECHO mission was able to take place and western humanitarian agencies have greater access to the area. The conflict nevertheless continues and we still have considerable concerns. In particular, we want to see much greater access for humanitarian aid agencies. We want to see genuinely independent investigation into reports of human rights abuses, and we want to see a real dialogue between the Russian government and the Chechens.

Step 2

The exercise is now to ignore all the padding and additional information and to identify the essential Subject Verb (Object) units that make up the backbone of the speech and separate them from one another...for example by hitting the return key twice between each section. By way of demonstration I have marked the Subject Verb and Object in each sentence. The first Subject Verb Object group is....

S   V

In the areas for which I have some responsibility, **there were** also, as the

O

Prime Minister has mentioned, some important **developments** at Feira.

    →   **There were... developments**

The second unit is,

S   V   O
We took stock of the European Union's **relations** with Russia and
O
the situation there, including in Chechnya, in the light of the recent EU-Russia Summit, which I think was regarded as fairly successful.

    →   **We... took stock of** ... **relations** (with Russia) and **the situation**.

If we continue to do the same throughout the passage we might arrive at the following. Notice that the "sections" or "sentences" range in length from 4 - 23 words, but each contains only one SVO unit, only one idea.

S   V

In the areas for which I have some responsibility, **there were** also, as the Prime

O

Minister has mentioned, some important **developments** at Feira.

S   V   O   O

We took stock of the European Union's **relations** with Russia and **the situation** there, including in Chechnya, in the light of the recent EU-Russia Summit, which I think was regarded as fairly successful.

S V   O

It is too early to judge President Putin's economic programme;

                  S   V   O

however, our basic **message is** that **a sound programme will be vital to boost investor confidence**.

           S   V

On Chechnya, **there have**, it is true, **been** some recent moderately positive

      O

developments in response to international and European Union pressure:

                 S   V   O

for example the recent **ECHO mission was able to take place**

                 S   V   O

and western humanitarian **agencies have greater access** to the area.

    S   V

The conflict nevertheless **continues**

     S   V   O

and **we** still **have** considerable **concerns**.

         S   V   O

In particular, **we want to see** much **greater access** for humanitarian aid agencies.

   S   V   O

We want to see genuinely independent **investigation** into reports of human rights abuses,

    S   V   O

and **we want to see** a real **dialogue** between the Russian government and the Chechens.

You may have noticed a subordinate clause tucked into this passage which appears not to fit into our SVO set up here. Don't worry about clauses for the moment. Clauses are very common in all types of speech but for the moment we want to concentrate only on the core message, the Subject Verb Object group. We will return to clauses like this at the end of Chapter 3.

Exercise

Now try to do the same yourself with the speech below. Copy the speech from the web address given at the back of the book (Example 8, page 228) into your word-processing software, remove the paragraph breaks to obtain the text as one block. Then read it and hit the return key twice after each SVO group.

This is a speech (henceforth **MacShane 1**) given by Denis MacShane, UK Minister for Europe on 8th October 2003 at the Atlantic Club in Sofia, Bulgaria. The Atlantic Club is a non-governmental organization which supported NATO accession for Bulgaria and fosters Euro-Atlantic values. Denis MacShane's parents are Polish emigrés, he speaks Polish and made many trips to Poland before and after the events of 1989. He is speaking in the context of Bulgaria's attempts to join the EU and after Bulgaria's accession to NATO.

> I am delighted to be back here in Sofia. The first time I came to Bulgaria was 20 years ago and then I never dreamed I would return as a UK government minister. Let me explain. In 1980 and 1981 I was heavily involved in supporting the independent Polish Union, Solidarność. In 1982 I was arrested and imprisoned in Warsaw when taking money to the underground activists of the union – men and women who today occupy high places in the national life of Poland. When I was released I was declared persona non grata by the communist government. I could not get a visa for Poland. My friends struggling for Polish freedom could not travel to the West. But we could both travel visa free to Varna. So on the sands of the Black Sea, the contacts were re-established, and over a glass of the wonderful wine that Bulgaria has the genius to produce, my footnote in the history of Europe's liberation from communism continued to be written. Now I am glad to be back in Bulgaria as a new generation of Bulgarian and British European citizens prepare to shape a new Europe. I am especially pleased to be speaking to you under the auspices of the Atlantic Club. Tony Blair, Bill Clinton, my friend the NATO General Secretary George Robertson, Mikhail Gorbachev and the Dalai Lama have all spoken here. It is an honour to follow in their footsteps, just as it is an honour to recall the memory of Major Frank Thompson, the poet and brother of one of England's greatest historians, E. P. Thompson. Frank Thompson parachuted into Bulgaria in 1944 as an SOE operative but was captured and executed. He sacrificed his life for Bulgaria and I recall his name tonight. The Atlantic Club has of course played a key role in pushing Bulgaria towards NATO accession. As the date of accession draws ever closer, I wonder however whether it is time for the Club to adopt a new slogan. The one in front of me/below me (on a banner, saying "NATO Accession NOW!") seems so successful, it appears rather outdated. Perhaps it is time to consider something else? "A Functioning and Effective Judiciary NOW!" would go down well just now in Europe's capital, Brussels, but it doesn't quite have the same ring to it. I would offer a new slogan "Let's Europeanize the Balkans before we Balkanize Europe!" Because the story of Europe in the lifetime of Europeans born since the end of the Second World War is little short of amazing. Our parents and grandparents grew up in a Europe that knew mainly violence, repression, emigration, religious intolerance and grinding poverty. For too many Europeans, life was nasty, brutish and short of nearly everything

today's European Union guarantees its citizens. To be sure, a European elite enjoyed high art, great literature and the chance to shine as officers on the field, gentlemen of the court, men of money or professors in the academy. But from 500 BC when the term Europe was first used - Europa was actually a maiden taken to the shores of Turkey to be ravished - until 1989, our continent failed rather than provided for its peoples. And today? The changes, even since 1973, when Britain entered the European Economic Community, are remarkable: The Europe of 1973 with its border control on goods and cars has gone. The myriad of currencies and currency controls acting as a blockage to fair, transparent, effective business has been replaced by a single market. One where the majority of EU citizens sensibly use one currency - the Euro. The Europe of 1973 with dirty beaches, and expensive air travel and telephone calls has been replaced by a Europe which allows more people to travel, talk to each other and enjoy a shared and better-protected natural environment than ever before. But perhaps most importantly, the division of the Europe of 1973 into communist, fascistic and democratic zones has all but disappeared. For the first time in European history a century opens up in which war, hunger, political oppression and fear are not the lot of the majority of European citizens. Europe has come a long way. But now is not the time to look back and marvel at what we have achieved. We need to look forward: beyond the fifteen current Member States and beyond even the ten countries joining the EU next May. Our primary objective should be to make sure that Europeans across the continent share in this progress. This means making a success of the first wave of accession in 2004. But equally importantly, it means maintaining the momentum of the process and looking ahead to the next milestone - and Bulgaria's accession together with Romania in 2007.

Now compare your version with your colleagues' and the version at the back of the book (page 212). Remember, the version at the back is not the "right" version, it is a version of what you might come up with.

How to practise

The practice exercises for this chapter are for transcripts only. You will skip this chapter when you work through the book with the spoken word. If you don't have access to a computer or the Internet you can skip these exercises and work through the next chapter, but be sure to spend a little longer practising the technique described there to make up for not being able to practise here.

If you do have access to a computer and the Internet, practise a lot!

1. Download transcripts of speeches from the Internet. Remember to ensure you find the type of speech that is interpreted in consecutive mode.

2. Copy the speeches into your word-processing software and remove all the paragraph breaks, or blank lines within the speech, as we did above. If necessary re-format the whole text so that you have single spacing between lines. You should now have a single block of text.

3. Now go through the speech with the cursor and hit the return key twice after each Subject Verb Object group; in other words, between ideas.

4. Print the result and compare with your colleagues. Do you agree on the divisions?

5. Repeat with more transcripts.

Chapter 3   The Beginning of Notes

"Separate the different parts of the message (which often correspond to sentences), using horizontal lines."

In this chapter we will turn the breakdown of the source text that we saw in Chapter 2 into a first attempt at note-taking. Each Subject Verb Object unit described in Chapter 2 is going to become a section of our notes, and each section will be separated from the next by a horizontal line across the page. On one page of your notepad you will have room for two, perhaps three, sections of notes, in which you note the Subject, Verb and Object diagonally across the page. Don't try to squeeze more than this onto a page, your notes will only become more difficult to read back. For this, start by using the boxes supplied below then for further practice get yourself a 10 x 15 cm spiral bound reporter's notepad.

The page will look something like this....

	Subject
	Verb
	Object
	——————
	Subject
	Verb
	Object
	——————

Whether you draw the horizontal line across the whole page, or only part of the page is simply a matter of personal preference. Some interpreters do, some don't. You will choose for yourself. The margin left free at the left hand side will be discussed in the next chapter. Don't worry about it for now.

Why note diagonally across the page?

In addition to reflecting our division between ideas, notes taken across the page like this have a number of advantages:

❑ **EASIER TO READ BACK:** because there is less writing on a page, so the ideas stand out on the page.

❑ **VISIBLE STRUCTURE**: the structure of the speech is visible at a glance. Something quite impossible if we note horizontally as we write normally.

❑ **EYES MOVE FROM LEFT TO RIGHT** in a natural movement, a little like a typewriter, always coming back to the left at the end of each idea.

❑ **THE BEGINNING OF EACH IDEA**, which is also often the most important part of it, is noted furthest to the left on the page, so we see it first. (This pattern will be looked at in more detail in Chapter 5).

❑ **NO SYNTACTIC INTERFERENCE:** something that horizontal notes encourage. That means using the wrong word order in the target language because you noted something in the source language word order.

❑ **SPACE FOR ADDITIONS**: in Chapter 8 we look at some of the detail you might need to add.

NB If you are working from a language where the word order is not necessarily Subject Verb Object, you can still note in this order. In German or the Slavic languages the inversions in word order are just stylistic so recreating the underlying SVO order on your notepad will make the notes clearer and interpreting easier.

Example

Step 1

Let's take the passage from Chapter 2 (**Patten**), split into sections as it was there.

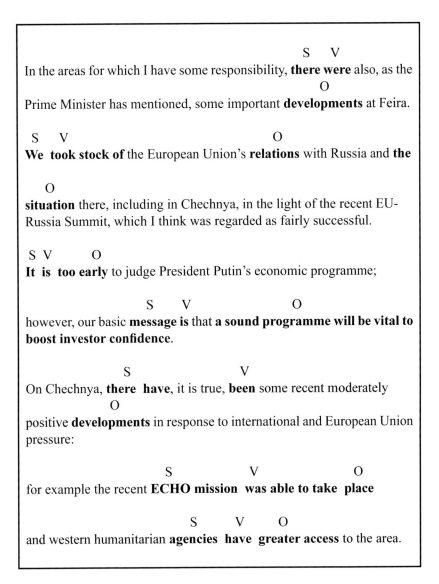

It is going to be crucial here, and during the rest of your interpreting career, to be able to fish the core ideas out of a more detailed source speech. Here because we are only just getting started we cannot be expected to get everything right, but what we want to commit to the notepad is the basic skeleton of the speech, the Subject Verb Object arrangement for each of the ideas expressed. The temptation will always arise to try and note everything down. RESIST IT!

Later we will not be able, nor will we want, to note all of what we hear, but we will be able to recall much of the detail from a speech thanks to the structured notes we have taken. That structure comes from first having heard and established what is the most basic message of a source text. That is what we are doing in this chapter.

Step 2

The first four sections of **Patten** might look like this,

	there	
		were
			developments
	_____	
we		
	took stock	
		relations
		+ situation
	_____	

it		
	is	
		too early
	_____	
message		
	is	
		good program = boost

The detail that you have not noted may come back to you when you look at the basic structure you have noted. But if it doesn't, don't worry. At this stage we are not trying to get everything right, we just want the main ideas.

For example, at this stage it would be a mistake to note the *economic programme* and not the *too early* because it is *too early* which makes the point, without it the rest is meaningless. If you ask yourself, *too early for what?*, you will probably be able to remember the detail, that it is too early *to judge the economic programme*. Note *economic programme* and you are less likely to make any association.

Look at the diagram on the next page. Note also in practice we rarely note things like *it is* and *there are* as above, but in these first demonstrations I have and you should too. Soon, though, you can do as most professionals do and simply note *developments* or *too early* alone, it will be clear to you what the verb was. If you do want to note the verb *to be* it will often be useful to use the =symbol.

The notes *developments* and *too early* then shift left in our notes. (See diagram on the next page.) This is the obvious practical thing to do if we stop noting *there are* etc.
See also Chapter 5 for more on positioning of notes on the page.

developments

———————

we

took stock

relations
+ situation

———————

too early

———————

message

=

good program = boost

Exercise

Try to make notes in the same way for the rest of the passage in the space below...

> On Chechnya, there have, it is true, been some recent moderately positive developments in response to international and European Union pressure: for example the recent ECHO mission was able to take place and western humanitarian agencies have greater access to the area. The conflict nevertheless continues and we still have considerable concerns. In particular, we want to see much greater access for humanitarian aid agencies. We want to see genuinely independent investigation into reports of human rights abuses, and we want to see a real dialogue between the Russian government and the Chechens.

Compare your notes with those of your colleagues. Do you agree on the breakdown? Remember, there is no one absolutely right answer to any of the questions consecutive poses, and so it can be very useful to compare with other students and your teachers to see how they tackle the same problems.

Below is an example of how those notes might have looked. They are neither complete, nor are they supposed to be at this stage, but they do offer the interpreter the basic structure of the speech. As we will see later, this can help us to note what's left more clearly without obscuring the central ideas or, even better, allow us not to note what is left and help us recall it from memory.

developments

—————————

ECHO mission

took place

—————————

agencies

have

more access

—————————

conflict

continues

—————————

we

concerned

—————————

we

want

more access for agencies

—————————

we

    want

        independent
        investigations

       ————————

we

    want

        real dialogue

      ————————

You can see how incomplete these notes are compared to the full text, but look at them again. Is there any doubt in your mind about the missing information? Try to answer the following questions using only these notes and see if the structure has helped you remember the information that we did not note above.

> We took stock of relations with whom, and the situation, where?
> Too early to judge what?
> A "sound programme" for what?
> Developments in Chechnya as a result of what?
> What type of agencies have more access?
> Independent investigations into what?
> Dialogue between who and who?

You don't have to have answered all these questions correctly to demonstrate that already at this early stage your memory is really quite good when it is given the RIGHT PROMPTS. Those prompts are to found in CONSISTENT AND STRUCTURED NOTES.

There will be a closer look at this function of notes in Chapter 7.

How to practise

Practise first with the transcripts of speeches, not the spoken word.

1. Repeat steps 1-3 from How to Practise in the previous chapter (page 41).

2. Now note each of the SVO elements from each section on a notepad, drawing a horizontal line across the page after each SVO group. Do not try to get all the detail at this stage, only the Subject Verb Object group as described in this chapter.

3. Compare with your colleagues. Do you agree on the divisions and notes?

4. Repeat with the transcripts of more speeches.

When you have worked through Chapter 4 and the section Moving On..., you will be ready to practise from the spoken word.

5. Follow the guidelines in Moving On... on giving speeches for your fellow students. To practise, simply listen to a speech given by a fellow student and note only the SVO groups on your notepad page.

> When you are comfortable with technique described in this chapter and have spent some time practising it turn to Part II, Clauses (page 125), for a look at how to deal with a frequently occurring sentence structure – the clause.

> Don't try to take in too much new information at once, but now might be a good time to dip into Part II and look at the Rules of Abbreviation (page 130).

> **Not noting the word**
>
> In the same way as you have begun to break down the speech into its basic units, now is the time to start thinking about the words used to represent each Subject, Verb and Object in the original. You are not obliged to use the same words in your notes as the speaker uses in their version. In fact it will be very useful if you can note something shorter but synonymous. Shorter to save time; synonymous, to avoid being trapped into using a word similar to the word the speaker has used, when it may not be appropriate, or worse it may be just plain wrong, in target language. (For example, despite appearances *eventuellement* in French is not the same as *eventually* in English.)
>
> This is the second way the word "idea" is used by interpreters (see Chapter 2, page 36) - to mean the underlying meaning of a word used. I will call this *concept* in this book. The following text is

the first and last word on the subject, culled from Rozan's *Note-taking in Consecutive Interpreting*. To avoid confusion over the use of the word "idea" as described in Chapter 2 I have doctored Rozan's text and replaced the word *"idea"* with the words *"underlying meaning"* where necessary.

"Take any French text and give it to 10 excellent English translators. The result will be ten very well translated texts, but ten very different texts in as far as the actual words used are concerned. The fact that we have ten good translations, but ten different texts, shows that what is important is the translation of the [underlying meaning] and not the word. This is even truer of interpretation since the interpreter must produce a version of the text in another language immediately. He must be free of the often misleading constraints that words represent. It is through the analysis and notation of the [underlying meaning] that the interpreter will avoid mistakes and a laboured delivery.

Example: Let us take the following, from French into English: *"Il y a des fortes chances pour que...../ There is a very good chance that...".* If we base our notation of this expression on the words, the key word is *chance.* If we base it on the [underlying meaning], it is *probable.*

The notes will have to be read 20 minutes – even an hour – after the idea was originally expressed. In the first example it would be very easy to make a mistake. Having noted *chance* the interpreter might, if the context allowed, render *"there is a chance that"* or *"by chance".* If on the other hand he noted *probable* the mistake cannot be made.

Example: *"We should try to live up to....".* It would be absurd to note the word *"live"* and it would greatly increase the risk of making a mistake. Although it would seem to be very different from the original it would be more appropriate to note in French, for example, *" à la hauteur"* (in English 'to be up to'). This is the result of analysing the [underlying meaning] behind what is said and noting it idiomatically in the target language. It would be just as useful to note *be =,* representing being equal to, which could very easily be read back idiomatically in interpretation (ie "à la hauteur in French", "to be up to in English").

Rozan, 2003:16 [1956:14]

These two skills: working out the basic meaning of a part of the original speech in terms of "Who does what to whom", in other words, what is the

Subject Verb and Object group, together with an ability to identify the underlying meaning below the veneer of the words chosen will be all important in your work as an interpreter working in consecutive mode.

Chapter 4   Links

In the previous chapter we looked at identifying ideas and used the Subject Verb Object group as our basic unit. Identifying the ideas is a major step towards understanding and recreating a speech as an interpreter, but just as important as the ideas themselves are the relationships between them: the links. Links signal the way the speaker wants the listener to relate what is about to be said to what has been said before (Baker, 1992:190). A speech is all about two things: the ideas and the links between them.

Why are links important? Let's look at some very straightforward examples.

> 1. The economy is struggling. The Central Bank has left interest rates unchanged.

In this example we have two ideas, represented by two SVO groups but we have no link between them. The ideas form a list of factual statements perhaps, but with no links between they are tell us very little. But what happens if there are links between the ideas?

> 2. The economy is struggling. However, the Central Bank has left interest rates unchanged.

We now have a very different message. See how much more these ideas say than Example 1. The links bring the ideas into relation with one another AND in doing so implicitly give us more information about the situation. In this example we are led to believe that the Central Bank had been expected to change interest rates (and basic economics suggests downwards) but that it has not done so.

But what if a different type of link had been used?

> 3. The economy is struggling. Consequently, the Central Bank has left interest rates unchanged.

In Example 3 the situation is the opposite. The Bank, we infer, would normally have raised its rate, for one reason or another, but because of the economic situation it did not (in order not to stifle growth, for example).

A speech without links is a meaningless list of ideas - and this, by the way, is why we have not tried to reproduce speeches from our notes before now. In this chapter we will try to identify some links and the words and expressions that are used to represent them and also develop a technique for noting them that reflects their importance within a speech. When we have done this we can move on to reproducing speeches from our notes. We'll do all this in a number of steps.

Step 1

Look at the text below. Which ideas are linked to one another and what words are used to represent that link?

Example (**Torry 1**)

> Britain and Germany are among those countries pushing most for an ambitious new WTO round. So, for both the UK and Germany, the failure of the trade talks in Cancun was a huge disappointment. A successful trade round would be a massive prize. If we could halve world tariffs, [then] that would add as much as $400 billion annually to world incomes, of which at least 150 billion will flow to developing countries. That's more than 3 times what they currently get in aid. But to achieve this we need to reform the CAP.

It is easier if we first split the text into SVO groups as we would have in the previous chapter. The links between the ideas are highlighted.

1	Britain and Germany are among those countries pushing most for an ambitious new WTO round.
2	**So**, for both the UK and Germany, the failure of the trade talks in Cancun was a huge disappointment.
3	A successful trade round would be a massive prize.
4	**If** we could halve world tariffs,
5	**[then]** that would add as much as $400 billion annually to world incomes, of which at least 150 billion will flow to developing countries.
6	That's more than 3 times what they currently get in aid.
7	**But** to achieve this we need to reform the CAP.

Idea 2 is a consequence of idea 1. The word that shows that link is *so*. Idea 5 a consequence conditional on Idea 4. Idea 7 is a counter argument to 4, 5 and 6. The speaker has left Idea 3 without any specific link to the other ideas, although clearly it is not out of place where it is. The speaker probably felt that the lack of link served to make the statement more emphatic.

Exercise

The text below is taken from the same speech (**Torry 1**).

Download the text from the site given on page 227, paste it into a word-processing file and begin by splitting the ideas in the same way as we did in Chapter 2. Then highlight the links as in the example above. Remember, not all ideas are linked and links don't necessarily come at the beginning of the sentence.

> You all know that the British Government would like to join the euro once the five economic tests are met.
>
> But selling the decision to the British public in a referendum will be difficult,
>
> if the eurozone economies, with Germany at the head, are seen to be performing badly.
>
> If on the other hand they are undertaking structural reforms which are dealing with the problems they face,
>
> promoting the euro in the UK is a much easier task.

Compare your version with your colleagues' and the version on page 216.

Step 2

Using the transcripts of speeches you have been using in Chapters 1-3 and any other suitable speeches you have found on the Internet, find as many different words and expressions that are used to link ideas as you can and write them into the box below.

Again compare with your colleagues' versions and try to arrive at as complete a list as possible.

Step 3

a) You will notice that many of the words you have come up with are very similar in meaning to one another. For example, *however* and *on the other hand*. Both express contradiction. Using the words and expressions you have found above, create groups of words with similar meanings - words and expressions which represent the same type of link. Jones calls these "families of links" (2002:53). Put each group in a box in the central column below.

b) In the column below on the right, try to describe the type of link that the words and expressions in the centre column represent - is it "cause and effect", "contradiction", "purpose"? The first one has been done by way of example.

	however, nonetheless, on the other hand, in spite of this etc.	contradiction

Step 4

Now try to come up with one short word or a clear and simple symbol to represent each group of words and put it in the box opposite that group in the left hand column above. This should be something clear and meaningful to you, not to your colleague, not to me or to a teacher, but to you, because this is the word or symbol you are going to use in your notes when working in consecutive.

One type of link can be represented by many words and expressions in the speaker's original, but as they are still the same type of link we only need note them in one way. If all contradictions are noted as *but* then you are distilling the original message down to its simplest form, your notes will be clear, and when you interpret the speech you will be able to choose from the many expressions in the target language that can express "contradiction" without being tied down by the speaker's version. This is the practical application of the mantra that we met earlier - "note underlying meanings (ideas) not words".

Example

Remember there is no one right way to do things, and this is not an exhaustive list of links or link words. Nor should you feel obliged to use the symbols proposed here. But they serve as examples. To make the groups I use clearer I've added a brief explanation of the common denominator in each group in the third column. I also have included the very important antithesis of a link - the lack of a link, which interpreters should note for themselves equally clearly.

B	*but, however, nonetheless, on the other hand, in spite of this, all the same,*	limitation or contradiction following an idea
THO	*although, despite (the fact that), even though, while, whilst, notwithstanding,*	limitation or contradiction preceding both linked ideas
COS	*because, the main reason for this, what is causing this, what's behind this?*	effect → cause
→	*hence, this means that, the result of this is, the consequence of this is, so that, because of this, therefore, this is why, not surprisingly then,*	cause → effect
TO	*(in order) to, in such a way as to, so that, with the aim of, the purpose being to,*	purpose

IF... →	*if .....then... (or inversion of same), had I known, were this to happen (and other similar conditionals), provided that, given a... then b*	condition and consequence
eg	*For example, in particular, i.e., e.g., amongst other things, inter alia, like, not least the,* and for announcing lists,	examples of the preceding idea - often in the form of lists
+	*also, in addition, and, not only, on top of that there is, furthermore*	addition
//	*The paragraph mark: no link, end of section, end of idea.*	no link

> You may well be following a university course in interpreting or have read other books about interpreting, in which case you will probably have heard the term "link words" several times already. You may also have come across the technical term "conjunctions". In fact both are a little deceptive. The former because it is not the words but the links themselves that interest us, the latter because a conjunction is not exactly the same thing as a link.
> What the interpreter wants to identify are the links the speaker sees between ideas, not the words or expressions used to signal them. For more on this have a look at Part 2, Implicit Links (page 147).

Step 5

We will take the text below and split it according to our work in Chapter 2 into SVO units. Using the information above, identify and highlight links between SVO units (if there is one) , then write the symbol that corresponds to that link (from your table above in Step 4.) in the left hand margin of the page. If there is no link between two ideas note that there is no link. The symbol *//* (denoting a new paragraph in the correction of written work) is clear and easy to remember but please choose any symbol that you are comfortable with.

> Why note the links on the left of the page?
>
> ❑   **VISIBILITY**: Things in the margin stand out. Links are important so we want them to stand out. This will help us later when we give back the speech. It is also an idea to note links slightly larger than your other notes for the same reason.
>
> ❑   **READABILITY**: The SVO groups together with the margin help the eyes to come back to the left hand side of page to start each new idea with its link to the previous one (like the motion of an old fashioned typewriter)*. This makes fluent production easier.
>
> * or right to left if you are noting in a language that reads in that direction.

Example (Torry 1)

Britain and Germany are among those countries pushing most for an ambitious new WTO round. So, for both the UK and Germany, the failure of the trade talks in Cancun was a huge disappointment. A successful trade round would be a massive prize. If we could halve world tariffs, [then] that would add as much as $400 billion annually to world incomes, of which at least 150 billion will flow to developing countries. That's more than 3 times what they currently get in aid. But to achieve this we need to reform the CAP.

//	Britain and Germany are among those countries pushing most for an ambitious new WTO round.
→	**So**, for both the UK and Germany, the failure of the trade talks in Cancun was a huge disappointment.
//	A successful trade round would be a massive prize.
if	**If** we could halve world tariffs,
then	**[then]** that would add as much as $400 billion annually to world incomes, of which at least 150 billion will flow to developing countries.
//	That's more than 3 times what they currently get in aid.
BUT	**But** to achieve this we need to reform the CAP.

Exercise

The text of the speech below (**Torry 1**) has been split into SVO units. Now highlight the links and note the corresponding symbol in the margin on the left of the box.

I don't believe that common rules across the EU are a solution to everything.
Different countries have different systems and structures, so a solution which works in one place will not necessarily work in another.
It doesn't make sense to regulate everything from Brussels.
But it does make sense to share our experience and to learn from each other.
Look for example at Germany and Britain. In Britain we envy Germany's training system for example. Or the high productivity of its workers. We can learn from Germany's successes here.
And in Britain we have had successes too.
Getting the long term unemployed back into work has been a major success.

	I don't believe that common rules across the EU are a solution to everything.
	Different countries have different systems and structures,
	so a solution which works in one place will not necessarily work in another.
	It doesn't make sense to regulate everything from Brussels.
	But it does make sense to share our experience and to learn from each other.
	Look for example at Germany and Britain.
	In Britain we envy Germany's training system for example. Or the high productivity of its workers.
	We can learn from Germany's successes here.
	And in Britain we have had successes too.
	Getting the long term unemployed back into work has been a major success.

Compare with colleagues' versions and the version on page 216.

You can see from the version at the back that different words representing the same link are noted with the one symbol only. That symbol is taken from the table of links above (*so* becomes →). Our notes no longer suggest a word to us, so during the production phase we are free to choose from all the possible synonymous expressions we know. This makes it easier to create a natural version in the target language.

Also the words and the links are not necessarily the same thing. In the second and third ideas (sentences) from the end it should be clear that there is an implicit *therefore* before *we can learn* and that the *AND* is not really bringing the two ideas together as a list but rather showing the division of the paragraph into two separate parts, one about Germany, one about the UK. Noting **+** might even lead to a mistake in interpretation here. Spotting links then, is not just about spotting link words. They can help us sometimes, but they are not always the same. When you have completed this chapter and practised this technique, turn to Part II, Implicit Links (page 147) for more on this.

Step 6

Replace the text with notes. That is, do with the text what we did in Chapter 3. Note the Subject, Verb and Object unit diagonally across the page. Note only the bare bones, the core message, the essentials. Using the same passage, I have done the first sentence by way of example, and the links (or lack of them) are already marked. So just add your SVO notes in the boxes below.

Exercise

1. If you are using your own notepad, draw a vertical line (about 3 cm from the left of the page) down each page. Otherwise use the box below.

2. Now make notes, in your pad or in the space provided, of the same text following the SVO pattern from Chapter 3.

The text is from the same speech as above. (**Torry 1**).

I

not think

∩
common rules

= panacea
_____

S

V

O

_____

→ S

V

O

_____

// S

V

O

_____

BUT	S
	V
	O
	—————
eg	S
	V
	O
	—————

//	S
	V
	O
	—————
→	S
	V
	O
	—————

//	S
	V
	O
	——
eg	S
	V
	O
	——

Now compare with colleagues and with the version on page 217.

How to practise

1. Keep practising steps 1, 3, 5 and 6 above with texts of speeches in your mother tongue (that you have downloaded from the Internet).

Step 1	- split a text into SVO units and highlight the links.
Step 3	- keep adding to your list of synonymous expressions for links.
Step 5	- split a text into SVO units and add symbols or words denoting the links between ideas in the left-hand margin.
Step 6	- when taking notes (diagonally across the page as in Chapter 3) add symbols or words denoting the links between ideas in the left-hand margin.

> Each time you start a new notepad go through it drawing a margin down the left-hand side of every page. This will save you time when practising and working and get you used to the presence of the margin on the page.

2. Then try the same with texts in a foreign language. Compare your work with other students or ask your teacher for advice.

3. Repeat the exercises with several speeches each day. Compare your notes with colleagues and look through them yourself. Can you improve on them? Rewrite them in "fair copy" from time to time, as this will help ingrain good habits in your note-taking technique.

4. To practise for this chapter using spoken speeches you will need to read the next section, Moving On... Then, from speeches given by your fellow students, try to note the SVO groups and the links. Make an effort to note only this and not to be tempted into noting details and forgetting these basics.

> When you have practised the ideas in this chapter and are comfortable with them turn to Part II, Uses of the Margin (page 137) to see what other uses the margin has when taking notes.

Moving On...

You have now reached an important stage in the progression towards a note-taking system. You have now met and practised the fundamentals of a note-taking system based on the notes of practising professionals. If you put this book down now and read no further, you will still be armed with a sound basis, tried and tested by many colleagues, for your future note-taking in consecutive interpreting. In this short chapter we will see how to move from noting from text to paper to the real thing. The chapter is divided into three parts:

- ❑ Taking notes directly
- ❑ Reproducing speeches from notes
- ❑ Note-taking from the spoken word

Taking notes directly

If you are comfortable with the techniques introduced so far and have practised them so that they come more or less automatically to you, you are now ready to take full notes directly, skipping the intermediate stages of Chapters 2, 3 and 4 and taking notes directly onto your notepad. There are a number of benefits to taking notes from texts of speeches before taking notes from the spoken word. There is no time pressure as with the spoken word, so you have more time to work out how you can best and most clearly note something. It also means you can correct as you go along, tear out a page and start it, but not the whole speech, again. This means that you will be practising what you would like to note, your ideal notes, your 'fair copy', not practising a hurried set of improvised notes. In turn this set of ideal notes will become ingrained through practice, and so when you do move on to noting from the spoken word the good habits will have become automatic and will find their way into your notes taken at speed.

Have a look at the example below, perhaps try to take some notes from it yourself before you look at my version. Remember, note only the Subject Verb Object unit and the link. Your memory will do enough of the rest for now.

After taking notes from a transcript go through them and "correct" them, try to improve them. Compare and discuss with a colleague how you tackled certain problems in the speech. Remember that there are no "right" or "wrong" notes, they must simply be clear to you, and often explaining them to colleagues will help you understand your own notes, their strengths and weaknesses, better.

Example (**Hodgson**)

But what I will tell you – and what a climatologist would tell you – is that this is what climate change looks like. One of the significant consequences expected from climate change is an increase in the frequency and severity of extreme weather events.

This is why we use the term climate change in preference to global warming, because it more accurately captures the range of climatic effects that the enhanced greenhouse effect is expected to produce. A long-term increase in global average temperatures is the key indicator and consequence of the build-up of greenhouse gases in the Earth's atmosphere. But the expected effects of that change on the world's climate systems are multiple and diverse.

The New Zealand dairy industry is founded on the superb conditions this country's climate provides for growing grass. This is why climate change matters to dairy farmers and – because of the economic importance of your industry – to New Zealand.

B	I
	will say
	∩ climate change
	= similar
	_____
//	1 result
	=
	more storms
	_____
→	we
	say
	"climate change"
	not "global warming"
	_____

cos	*this term*
	more accurate
	_____
//	*rising temperature*
	= *indicator + effect*
	_____
BUT	*effects*
	= *multiple + diverse*
	_____

//	*NZ dairy industry*
	based on
	great climate
	_____
→	*climate change*
	=
	impor ᵗ to farmers
	+ to NZ

Reproducing speeches from notes

You have probably been impatiently waiting for the moment when you start reproducing the speeches you are reading and taking notes from, not to mention listening to speeches rather than working with written texts. Since you now have the foundations of a system which will help you to do this we can make a start.

This step is very simple. Using the notes you have made from written texts as part of previous chapters and during your own practice - notes which include the Subject, Verb, Object units and the links between them - try to reproduce, orally, a version of the source speech, either in the same language or a target language, from these notes. Keep practising with other transcripts. This is the production phase of consecutive interpreting. By only starting with the production phase now, on the basis of structured notes produced from the written word you will have more time and mental resources available to work on your presentation skills in the production phase. Those skills are fluency, natural intonation, engaging your audience and using your notes correctly to do the above.

Now is also the moment to look at how to read back these notes. This is also going to make a difference to your performance when interpreting. In fact the word "read" might be misleading when we talk about using notes to recreate a speech because interpreters do not read their notes in the usual sense of the word. The best description of the technique interpreters should use to read back from their notes when interpreting consecutively is that given by Jones (2002:64), reproduced below. This is not a technique that you will master immediately, and with each new technique you learn in this book your presentation will probably suffer somewhat as you concentrate on what is new at the expense of other elements of your interpretation. With this in mind you might re-read the extract below at regular intervals just to make sure you haven't forgotten how to use your notes effectively.

> It may seem strange to even mention how to read back notes. However, interpreters should be aware of the risk of communicating less well because of looking too much at their notes and not enough at their audience. This risk is particularly great if the interpreter takes relatively complete notes. Interpreters, like public speakers, must learn the art of glancing down at their notes to remind them of what they are to say next and then delivering that part of the text while looking at the audience. The clearer the notes, both in content and lay-out, the easier this will be. And the clearer the ideas in the interpreter's mind, the more cursory the glances down at the notes can be.
>
> There is a specific technique that interpreters can try to develop, and which can be compared to a pianist reading music while playing but not sight-reading. The pianist who has practised a piece is in a similar situation to the consecutive interpreter: essentially they know what they

want to play but the sheet-music is there to remind them. The pianist looks at the opening bars and then starts playing, and continues reading ahead of the notes they are playing, their eyes on the music always being a little ahead of their fingers on the keyboard. Similarly the interpreter should look at the first page of their notes then start speaking while looking up at their audience. As the interpreter moves towards the end of the passage they have looked at, they glance down at their notes again to read the next passage. In other words they do not wait until they finished one passage to look again at their notes, which would mean that the interpretation would become jerky, reading then speaking, reading then speaking. Rather the interpreter, while still talking, is already reading ahead, preparing the next passage, thus providing for a smooth, uninterrupted and efficient interpretation.

Jones, 2002:64

When applying this technique you will notice that you are constantly reading ahead in your notes, but that at the bottom of each page your continuity is broken as you turn over to a new page. To avoid this inconvenience and the shock of not knowing what is coming on the next page, try turning your pages as described in the diagram below. This will be doubly useful as speakers are unlikely to break their speeches into notepad page size chunks for the benefit of the interpreter.

As you approach the bottom of the page use the finger and thumb of the hand not holding the pad to slide the page upwards. Keep the bottom half of the page flat on the pad and let the top half curl up into itself. This will reveal the top of the next page, while you can still see the bottom of the previous one. In this way you can turn page after page fluidly, reading ahead all the time, without ever being interrupted by the end of a page in your notes.

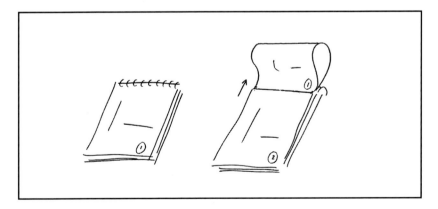

Figure 2

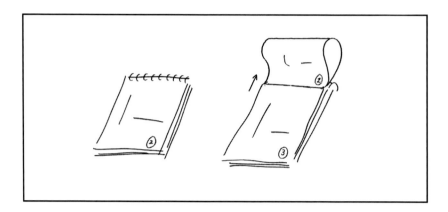

Figure 3

This technique is also the reason why most interpreters only note on one side of the page.

So now you have sets of notes, a note-taking technique that will allow you to prepare, create and/or reproduce speeches. This brings us on to...

Note-taking from the spoken word

The sets of notes that you now have can be used to give speeches for your colleagues during practice sessions. In this way you can move on from written texts to working with the spoken word. Giving speeches from your notes for colleagues to practise from, rather than using tapes or reading transcripts verbatim, is useful for a number of reasons,

1. One person has made a set of notes, which is a useful practice exercise of the skills outlined in the previous chapters. That person...
2. then gives a speech on the basis of those notes. This too is useful practice, this time in note-reading. It will become apparent whether or not your notes are clear to you when you try and do this.
3. Meanwhile your colleagues who, like you, are just beginning to work with the spoken word have a spoken source speech to interpret that has already been analysed once, and at this stage will be both simpler and clearer than the original it was taken from.
4. And because it is not an audio or video recording you won't need any equipment to practise, so you can practise anywhere.

Point 3 is particularly important as it avoids the unfortunate practice of students reading texts to one another. This should be avoided until the very final part of your course because,

1. Reading aloud is boring and offers no useful activity to the person reading.
2. Transcripts read aloud are usually read aloud badly, especially when unprepared. Intonation and variation of pace, essential indicators for the interpreter, are usually missing (Seleskovitch and Lederer, 2002:57). These additional difficulties, should only be introduced later on in your course, if at all.
3. Transcripts read aloud word for word are too dense to interpret consecutively at early stages in the course.
4. Speakers giving speeches in the sort of situation that might require consecutive interpretation (see Introduction, page 3) usually speak from notes and do not read texts verbatim.
5. All of the above reduce motivation levels, which helps no-one.

Taking notes from the spoken word is a different exercise to note-taking from transcripts. You will be doing things more quickly, and you will be noting and listening at the same time. This will require some practice, as we often forget to listen when we are concentrating on our note-taking. But we don't want or need to concentrate on the details of any speech at this stage. That will come later as you master the rest of this note-taking system and as your abilities as an interpreter develop. Your analytical skills and your memory will get better and better as you continue, so don't expect to get it all right now.

One thing will be the same though. With the transcript you had to read a whole chunk before noting anything useful. In the same way, you should listen to a whole "chunk" before noting anything. The temptation will be to write immediately you hear anything. DON'T!

Grading your material

It is important to work up slowly from easier to more difficult tasks. First work from (spoken speeches in) your mother tongue into your mother tongue, then when you are comfortable noting from the spoken word, from a foreign language into your mother tongue. And finally, if you work into a foreign language, practise working from your mother tongue into that foreign language.

1.	Mother tongue	→ Mother tongue
2.	Foreign source language	→ Mother tongue
3.	Mother tongue	→ Foreign language

This progression should take place over a number of weeks, not in the course of an afternoon. There is no need to rush, you have months or years to perfect these skills. That is also why I recommend that you start by giving speeches for each other, from notes you have taken, rather than using tapes and videos of speakers and politicians, which may be too difficult at these early stages.

The same applies to the level of difficulty of source material. Make sure you don't jump straight into working from very difficult speeches. Below is a series of graded steps for moving from simple to more difficult types of speech (Seleskovitch and Lederer 2002:77). If you rush into difficult speeches, you will try to note too much and lose the structure that you have been learning here because it is not yet automatic. As the method becomes more automatic you can move on to the next chapters of this book and the last two levels of the schema below.

1. Narratives on subjects you are familiar with.
2. Debates, for and against, on subjects you are familiar with.
3. Narratives on subjects you don't know much about.
4. Debates, for and against, on subjects you don't know much about.
5. Speeches in a high register of language on subjects you are familiar with.
6. Speeches in a high register of language on subjects you know little about.

Make sure you get lots of practice!

Chapter 5   Verticality§ and Hierarchies§ of Values

> Many a poor consecutive is sub-standard even though "everything is there", since everything is given the same weight and no particular elements or threads are highlighted, making it difficult for the listener of the interpretation to know what the speaker is really trying to say.
>
> Jones, 2002:22

In this chapter we look at four ways of reflecting in our notes the differing levels of importance (values) that the speaker has given to the elements of a speech. In learning to do this, we will learn to identify, note and through this communicate to the listener some of those same variations.

Any speaker will have more and less important things to say. Good speakers will vary the volume, speed and tone of their delivery to make these differences apparent to their audience. Interpreters will wish to do the same, but, unlike the speaker, they will be working not on the basis of their own convictions, but rather from what the speaker has said, their memory of the same and the notes they have made. Clearly then it is worth having a consistent system that will allow interpreters to see at a glance what is more and what is less important in the speech they are interpreting so that they too can offer the correct intonation, speed and volume. This is particularly important, although not only, in un-inflected languages.

Parallel values§

You may have noticed in the previous chapters that the notepad page has been divided more or less into four vertical columns. One of these, the margin, is visible because we draw it at the left of the page, and in it we note the links. The other three columns are virtual and in them we have been noting our Subject Verb Object groups, our ideas.

LINK	SUBJECT		
		VERB	
			OBJECT

Let us imagine that there are two Subjects for the same verb in one group. Until we are told differently we must assume that they are equally important, that they are of "equal value", in relation to the Verb and the Object. To represent this on the page they are noted on top of one another in the same (invisible) column. Let's look at an example. In the following basic sentence there is one element in each column.

Example

Because the French government have cut customs duties.

COS	Fra		
		cut	
			duties

Now imagine it had read,

Because the French, German and British governments have cut customs duties.

In this example, "French, German" and "British" are of equal "value". They are noted parallel to one another.

COS	Fra Ger UK		
		cut	
			duties

This technique, which is also known as "verticality" or "tiering[§]" and was first described by Jean-François Rozan (1956), holds up to any number of permutations and still offers the interpreter a clear picture of what is going on. If you try noting **Fra Ger UK** horizontally in your notepad you will see how much less clear it is on the page.

The same technique can be applied to the other columns if, for example there is more than one Verb or Object. If we expand the example further, we can see that the same system for note-taking can absorb any number of combinations. This will come in handy, as speakers often like to group things in threes for reasons of style.

> Because the French, German and British governments have cut customs duties, visa fees and administrative charges.

COS	Fra		
	Ger		
	UK		
		cut	
			duties
			visa fees
			admin charges

or...

> Because the French, German and British governments have cut, simplified or abolished customs duties, visa fees and administrative charges.

COS	Fra		
	Ger		
	UK		
		cut	
		simplified	
		OR abolished	
			duties
			visa fees
			admin charges

This technique is also useful for multiple adjectives. (Adjectives are best noted in the same virtual column as the noun they qualify). For example we could have noted the third example slightly differently...

> Because the French, German and British governments have cut customs duties.

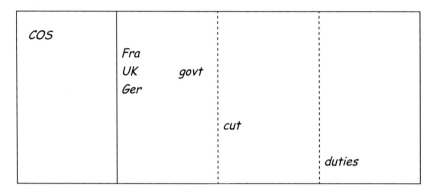

These examples are also a demonstration of the bottom-up approach that I mentioned in the introduction. That is that you may not have been aware of the idea of looking for hierarchies or parallels within the speech and consequently won't have seen them - now you are aware and you will start seeing these hierarchies more and more.

Example (**MacShane 1**)

> Now I am glad to be back in Bulgaria as a new generation of Bulgarian and British European citizens prepare to shape a new Europe. I am especially pleased to be speaking to you under the auspices of the Atlantic Club. Tony Blair, Bill Clinton, my friend the NATO General Secretary George Robertson, Mikhail Gorbachev and the Dalai Lama have all spoken here...

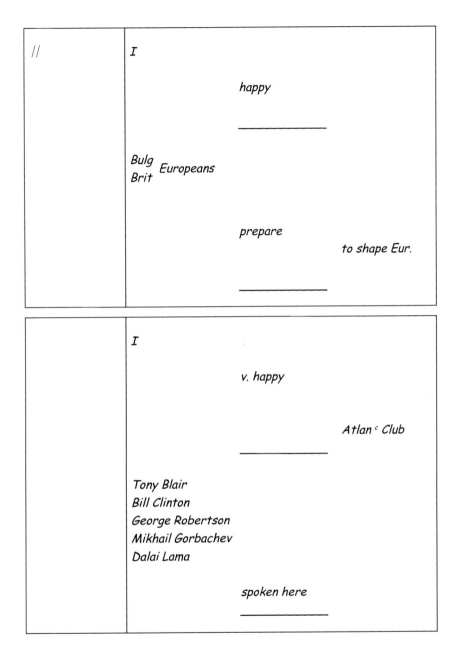

Exercise

Try noting the following passage in the boxes below or on your own note pad. Remember you are still not trying to note or reproduce everything, you are looking for the Subject Verb Object group, the links and now the hierarchies of value.

This speech (henceforth **Blair 2**) was given by the British Prime Minister, Tony

Blair, to the Confederation of Indian Industry, on 5th January 2002, in Bangalore, India. Bangalore is the motor of the Indian high-tech industry. The war on terror has begun and India has its own problems of violence in Kashmir and tensions between Hindu nationalists and India's Muslim minority. The full text is available at the URL given on page 228.

> Today, as well as our business and trade links, we are joining together in the fight against terrorism. I want to express our total solidarity with you in the face of recent terrorist outrages in India.
>
> There can be no room in any civilised society for organisations such as Lashkar e Toiba and Jaish Mohammed - groups banned by the British government some time ago. The appalling attacks on India's Parliament of 13th December and on the Jammu and Kashmir Assembly on 1st October demonstrate more clearly than ever the threat such fanatics pose not just to your democracy, but to all democracies - and to civilised values in the whole world.
>
> Of course, people are entitled to pursue their political views by legitimate means. But the indiscriminate and deliberate murder of civilians to cause chaos and mutilation defiles any political cause.

Compare with the version at the back of the book (page 220).

Shifting values[§]

The virtual division into columns that we have worked with in this chapter allows the interpreter working in consecutive mode certain freedoms which can be very useful in rendering a speech properly. The elements to be noted, (links, subjects, verbs and the like) can be shifted from the column to which they have been assigned until now, to the left or the right depending on what we want to achieve. Let us assume that the more important something is the further to the left of the page we note it. We can now give degrees of importance to elements by moving them (and everything that follows them in one section of notes) further from or nearer to the left hand side of the page.

First, if the Subject is particularly important, for example because the speaker is comparing what X is doing with what Y is doing, then the Subject (Verb Object) can be shifted left one imaginary column to emphasize the added weight the subject has.

Example (Torry 1)

I was looking recently at a survey of young people's attitudes in both countries.

Germans see the UK as a good place to work and to study - second only to the US. They recognise that we have a creative, multicultural society. But Germans see us as reluctant Europeans. They have the impression that we don't like them very much.

Young British people said they admired Germany's high-quality cars and its well-organised people. But they still associated Germany with the 12 years between 1933 and 1945.

So instead of noting...

Ger °

        think

∩

        etc etc etc
        ———————

UK °

        think

∩

...we can note...

```
Ger °
        think

        ∩                      etc etc etc
                               _____


UK°
        think

        ∩
```

The fact of our abbreviation for Germans and Britons being further to the left will announce its greater significance in the sentence, underline the fact that one is compared with the other and consequently make it easier for us to give it the corresponding intonation when we reproduce the speech.

Alternatively if the reasoning is secondary, of lesser importance, the link (and the SVO after it) might all shift to the right to represent lesser importance. Look at the example below.

Example (Patten)

On Chechnya, there have, it is true, been some recent moderately positive developments in response to international and European Union pressure.

According to our work so far this sentence could be noted as below...

```
              dev ᵗs

cos
              int ᴵ
              EU      pressure


                      _____
```

But, imagine that, having heard the speech, we think that the ***cos*** (*because*) is not a major link but rather a link to an additional but fundamentally secondary piece of information. In that case we note it and the elements of the idea that follow it further to the right as below...

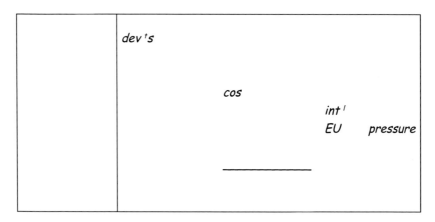

This system suggests that the most important elements are furthest to the left, and that any two elements in the same section of notes, the same idea, that are vertically aligned on the page are of equal value.

Exercise

Try the same with the text of the speech below (**Blair 2**) in the boxes provided or in your own notepad. Compare your notes with colleagues'.

> In part this is by virtue of our history. Our past gives us huge, perhaps unparalleled connections with many different regions of the world. We are strong allies of the US. We are part of the European Union. Our ties with the Commonwealth, with India and other parts of this sub-continent, are visibly strengthening. Similarly, our relations with the Middle East, with Russia and China, are all areas where we are enjoying a closer friendship than for many years.

Now compare with colleagues and with the version on page 221.

Parallel values 2

Once we have applied the techniques of Parallel and Shifting Values and learnt to position elements on the page according to their importance in the speech, we can assign value to whole sections of our notes by aligning their respective starting points with one another on the page, or on subsequent pages.

For example, it is not at all uncommon for speakers to have the same subject doing many different things, and with some distance between the repetitions of the subject or pronoun representing it. By noting the verbs parallel with one another on the page we see clearly that they have the same subject, thus we give the correct intonation to our rendering of the speech and we save considerable time in not noting the same thing several times.

Example (**Blair 2**)

For the purposes of this example I have highlighted the verbs that go with the subject *a successful economy*.

> First, any successful economy **needs to conform** to certain basics. It **should be** an open economy, willing to let capital and goods move freely. It **needs** financial and monetary discipline - the markets and investors swiftly punish the profligate. It **needs to encourage** business and enterprise - to create an enabling climate for entrepreneurs. A few years ago, people might have stopped there. But now we can add confidently: the successful economy also **must invest** heavily in human capital, technology and infrastructure. Education is a top economic as well as social priority. High levels of unemployment and social exclusion do not just disfigure society, they waste the national resource of human talent.

//

successful econ

must conform

certain basics

_____

should be

open

(let capital
+ goods move)

_____

needs

financ
monetary discipline

		encourage
		business + enterprise
|| Few years ago	would be	
		enough
BUT	now we <u>add</u>	
	successful econ	
		must invest
		human capital technology infrastructure

See how clear the comparison will be to us when reading back the notes because of the parallel positioning of the verbs.

Exercise

Try the same with the text below, taken from the same speech (**Blair 2**) by Tony Blair.

> That is why both Britain and India place such emphasis on it today, backed by businesses that know that without the skills, the economy cannot progress. This is the role of the enabling state. These rules are tough though. They require nations to open markets and that can be painful. And they require political leaders to fund investment where benefits may not be fully realised within the electoral cycle.

Now compare with colleagues and with the version on page 223.

Use of brackets

By positioning an element vertically below another, but in brackets, we can clearly identify that the one belongs to the other, but is subordinate to it within the clause or SVO group. As a result we can adjust our intonation appropriately when reproducing the speech from our notes.

***Example* (MacShane 1)**

> And today? The changes, even since 1973, when Britain entered the European Economic Community, are remarkable:

The SVO group is clearly, *the changes are remarkable*. This is the basic message of the sentence. But how do we note the secondary information so that when we read back the notes we see immediately what is the primary message and what is additional information?

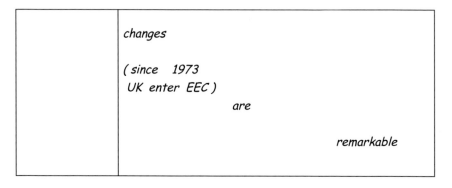

To do this well you need to have a very clear idea of what the basic message is, what the SVO group is. Let's look at the following text and work through it in 3 stages.

> And today? The changes, even since 1973, when Britain entered the European Economic Community, are remarkable:
> The Europe of 1973 with its border control on goods and cars has gone. The myriad of currencies and currency controls acting as a blockage to fair, transparent, effective business has been replaced by a single market. One where the majority of EU citizens sensibly use one currency - the Euro.
> The Europe of 1973 with dirty beaches, and expensive air travel and telephone calls has been replaced by a Europe which allows more people to travel, talk to each other and enjoy a shared and better-protected natural environment than ever before.

Step 1

First we break it down into Subject Verb Object groups. These are marked in bold.

And today? **The changes**, even since 1973, when Britain entered the European Economic Community, **are remarkable**:

The **Europe of 1973** with its border control on goods and cars **has gone**.

The **myriad of currencies and currency controls** acting as a blockage to fair, transparent, effective business **has been replaced by a single market**. One where the majority of EU citizens sensibly use one currency - the Euro.

The **Europe of 1973** with dirty beaches, and expensive air travel and telephone calls **has been replaced by a Europe** which allows more people to travel, talk to each other and enjoy a shared and better-protected natural environment than ever before.

Step 2

We find that there were relatively few basic SVO units, each with lots of secondary information attached to each element (the Subject, Verb or Object). Below I have used the full text of the speech but given it the layout that it could have on the note pad. The SVO unit is noted in normal font in bold, and the additional information, which we will note in brackets in the future, is below the element it belongs to in *italics*.

	The changes, *(even since 1973, when Britain entered the European Economic Community)*	**are**	**remarkable**
		_____	
	The Europe of 1973 *(with its border control on goods and cars)*	**has gone.**	
		_____	

The myriad of currencies and currency controls *(acting as a blockage to fair, transparent, effective business)*	**has been replaced**	
		by a single market. *(One where the majority of EU citizens sensibly use one currency - the Euro.)*
The Europe of 1973 *(with dirty beaches, and expensive air travel and telephone calls)*	**has been replaced**	**by etc.**

Note that if you only reproduced what is marked in bold above, you would still have a meaningful speech, that got across the same message as the original.

Step 3

This in turn might give us the following set of notes. (What was in italics above is now only between brackets.)

changes

(since 1973
UK enter EEC)

are

remarkable

———————

Europe 1973
(border controls)

has gone

———————

currencies +
curr   controls

(block
        fair
        transp [t]   bus [ns])
        effec [v]

replaced

by single market
(EURO)

———————

```
Europe 1973


        (     dirty     beaches
              expen ᵛ  air
                        phone   )



                              replaced


                                          by...
                        _____
```

Of course you must also use your own discretion about how the notes appear, and their clarity for your use. If the brackets do not fit snugly underneath the concept they are attached to then we can stretch them out across the page a little, as in the example above.

As interpreters working in consecutive mode it is neither possible nor desirable for you to note everything. But as you become familiar with this system and with what your own memory can do you will know what you can leave out and recall later and what you really need note. This is looked at in more detail in Chapter 7, Memory Prompts. Once again the structure should help you reconstruct the missing information. Can you answer the following questions from the notes above?

> Border controls on what?
> Complete the information that is represented by *(EURO)* above.
> What does *by...* represent?

With this in mind could you reproduce a version of this part of the speech from the notes above? Remember, you are not aiming for perfection yet.

Exercise (**MacShane 1**)

Repeat Steps 1-3 above with the next part of the same speech below. Or simply take notes directly from the text, using brackets to note information you consider not to be part of the SVO units that make up the basic message.

> The arguments for enlargement are well rehearsed, but I think it's worth reminding ourselves briefly of quite how important the process is to the future of the EU. In an age when most major issues affect continents, not countries, working on a European level is the only effective way to tackle them - for

current Member States and future Member States alike...

...And it is only collectively that we will be able to reap the benefits of a vast single market - larger than the US and Japan combined. An enlarged EU will increase trade and offer new opportunities for consumers. It is already stimulating new markets, new investment opportunities and new jobs.

Now compare with colleagues and the version on page 224.

How to practise

From this point on you may want to stop using the transcripts of speeches to practise from and work only with the spoken word. This is possible, but it is always easier to learn a new technique when you are not under the time pressure associated with taking notes from spoken speeches.

1. Download the texts of speeches from the Internet. Start with the texts of speeches in your mother tongue, later move on to speeches in a foreign langauge.

2. Make notes from the texts of the speeches using the techniques described in this chapter.

3. Before you start reproducing speeches from these notes, read through them. Are they clear? Can you see the structures described above, and will that help you to reproduce the original speech? Where you feel they are not clear, "correct" your notes, that is change them to how you would have written them in an ideal world – according to the techniques in this chapter. Correcting notes in this way is a useful exercise in helping to make the application of these techniques automatic.

4. Move on to spoken source speeches. Can you still structure your notes clearly under time pressure? Read through your notes and "correct" them. Compare and discuss with colleagues.

Chapter 6   Symbols

When note-taking is mentioned in the context of consecutive interpreting the first thing that student interpreters ask about are symbols. You have already seen or come up with a number of them in Chapter 4. Although it is true that knowing a reasonable number of very useful symbols can make our lives much easier, please don't forget that symbols are relatively unimportant when compared to all of what you have read in the first five chapters of this book. The note-taking system described here, variants on it and other note-taking systems work with or without symbols, but if you don't have a sound, consistent and meaningful note-taking system then no amount of symbols is going to help you.

In this chapter we look at some of the guiding principles that should govern your use of symbols in consecutive note-taking.

What is a symbol?

A symbol doesn't have to be a picture. It also can be a short word, pair of letters or a single letter. What is important is that it represents something. What does it represent? When noting with symbols it is the underlying meaning of a word or expression that is important to us, rather than the actual word or expression chosen by the speaker to represent that meaning (e.g. *suggest, propose, put forward*). We will call this underlying meaning **concept** here. So a symbol represents a concept, not a word. This is often what interpreters mean when they say "note the ideas [concepts], not the words!". (See Chapter 2, page 36).

Example

B   You can use a capital *B* to represent all contradictions, so not just *but*, but also, *however, nonetheless, on the other hand*, etc.

→   An arrow can be used to represent consequence. A leads to B. *Causes, therefore, as a result*, etc.

Why use symbols?

Symbols... ... are **quicker and easier** to write than words.
... are **easier to read** on the page that words.
... **represent concepts not words,** they are not one-to-one translations so they help us avoid source language interference when we interpret.

What to note with symbols

i) *Concepts that come up again and again*

In all sorts of speeches there are concepts and expressions that are the stock and trade of every speaker, things that come up every time. e.g. verbs like *agree, decide, discuss, propose,* or *consider*. Symbols for these concepts will be used again and again, every time you work in consecutive mode.

Exercise (**MacShane 1**)

Look at the speech below. Which ideas or synonymous expressions come up most often? And which would you expect to find in other speeches as well?

> I am delighted to be back here in Sofia. The first time I came to Bulgaria was 20 years ago and then I never dreamed I would return as a UK government minister.
>
> Let me explain. In 1980 and 1981 I was heavily involved in supporting the independent Polish Union, Solidarność. In 1982 I was arrested and imprisoned in Warsaw when taking money to the underground activists of the union – men and women who today occupy high places in the national life of Poland.
>
> When I was released I was declared persona non grata by the communist government. I could not get a visa for Poland. My friends struggling for Polish freedom could not travel to the West. But we could both travel visa free to Varna. So on the sands of the Black Sea, the contacts were re-established, and over a glass of the wonderful wine that Bulgaria has the genius to produce, my footnote in the history of Europe's liberation from communism continued to be written.
>
> Now I am glad to be back in Bulgaria as a new generation of Bulgarian and British European citizens prepare to shape a new Europe. I am especially pleased to be speaking to you under the auspices of the Atlantic Club.

The concept of "pleased" comes up three times in this section alone - *delighted, glad, pleased*. And it will also come up many times in other speeches, regardless of their content. It is worth having a quick symbol for all the expressions that mean "pleased". For example, ☺. Concepts like *imprisoned* or *arrested* are going to be rare in most contexts, so don't bother coming up with a symbol for it as you will only forget it through lack of use. Concepts like *support* or *government*, though, might come up in many other speeches.

Now do the same with other speeches in this book, or speeches you have worked with recently and complete the table below. Put frequently occurring words and their synonyms in the left column and a symbol for them in the right hand column. **Remember you want one symbol for a group of more or less synonymous words and expressions, NOT one symbol per word.**

Frequently occurring groups of more or less synonymous verbs

speak, say, announce, declare, tell etc.	*"*

Frequently occurring groups of more or less synonymous nouns

support, backing, endorsement	*S*

Many of the above may appear as both nouns and verbs. You will find that in this note-taking system you can use the same symbol for both verb and noun without any confusion. Below are a few examples of what you might have arrived at...

Frequently occurring VERBS

speak, say, announce, declare etc.	*"*
want, wish, desire, hope for,	♥

think, consider, hold the view, be minded to, be of the conviction,	$\tilde{O}$
propose, suggest, put forward, move to, nominate,	>>

Frequently occurring NOUNS

support, backing, endorsement, etc.	S
consequence, result, end-effect, ramifications, repercussions,	$\rightarrow$
problem, difficulty, hindrance, hurdle, stumbling block (which gives us this symbol),	$\wedge\wedge\wedge$
country,	
politics, policy,	Π
money,	$\$$
Industry (this symbol represents a chimney with smoke coming out of it),	Γ

Verbs or nouns

Some words, concepts and their symbols may function as nouns or verbs, but with the SVO layout on the page you cannot confuse their grammatical function.

support, backing, endorsement, etc.	S
decide, decision,	$\emptyset$
change, reform, overhaul, rework, redraft, amend,	Δ

Links belong to this category and will come up again and again in all speeches. See Chapter 4, page 60, for symbols for links.

ii)   *Ideas that will recur on a given day*

In any one meeting certain terms or concepts will be particular to that day's subject matter. This is a more practical point. If you are preparing to work at a meeting on competition in telecommunications services, it might be useful to have a symbol for "unbundling" or "last-mile" as these longish to write and may come up dozens of time in a debate on the subject. After the meeting has finished though, you may not need to use them again for weeks or even months as they will only come in the context of a discussion about telecommunications and interpreters work in many different subject areas.

Example

In the continuation of the speech above (**MacShane 1**) we have a good example. Denis MacShane, we know, is speaking to the Atlantic Club, in Bulgaria, about Bulgaria. The interpreter would be well advised to have considered this in advance and have prepared symbols for these two things in advance as they are likely to be mentioned repeatedly. Look at the example below.

> Now I am glad to be back in **Bulgaria** as a new generation of **Bulgarian** and British European citizens prepare to shape a new Europe. I am especially pleased to be speaking to you under the auspices of the **Atlantic Club**. Tony Blair, Bill Clinton, my friend the NATO General Secretary George Robertson, Mikhail Gorbachev and the Dalai Lama have all spoken here. It is an honour to follow in their footsteps, just as it is an honour to recall the memory of Major Frank Thompson, the poet and brother of one of England's greatest historians, E. P. Thompson. Frank Thompson parachuted into **Bulgaria** in 1944 as an SOE operative but was captured and executed. He sacrificed his life for **Bulgaria** and I recall his name tonight.
>
> The **Atlantic Club** has of course played a key role in pushing **Bulgaria** towards NATO accession. As the date of accession draws ever closer, I wonder however whether it is time for the **Club** to adopt a new slogan.

The symbols need not be pictorial and even something as simple as *AC* (Atlantic Club) and *Bu* (Bulgaria) will be clear and save you plenty of time.

How to use symbols

Symbols must be...

- **clear and unambiguous.**

- **quick and simple to draw.** You can categorize symbols by the number of strokes of the pen required to draw them. More than three is probably too slow.

- **prepared in advance**, and instantly familiar to you. Don't improvise mid speech.

- **consistent**, if *E* is *energy* today, make sure it stays *energy* always and find yourself another symbol for *environment* and *economy*. Otherwise you will mix them up and make some terrible mistakes.

- **organic**. See below for an explanation of organic symbols.

...and they must...

- **mean something to you**. Copying symbols from other people can be a good idea, but symbols work because they create associations in the mind, in your mind, and the human memory prefers you to understand those associations yourself. So don't blindly copy symbols you see here or elsewhere if they don't create the right associations for you, if they don't "click" for you.

Organic[§] symbols

"Organic" means that one symbol should be the starting point for many other symbols. A group or family of symbols will grow from a common root. In this way you will reinforce your recognition of the symbols you know and by having a smaller number of "basic" symbols you will tax your memory less. Both of these things will free up mental resources and help you interpret better.

Let's look at some examples. One of the most commonly used symbols is a simple square which denotes "country, nation, land, state", depending on the context. It has been borrowed from Japanese, where a similarly shaped character means "country". Using our square as a starting point, and by adding a couple of letters we can arrive at a whole range of symbols, with no extra effort required.

Nation, country, state = ☐

☐ *al*   national (adjective)

☐ *ally*   nationally

☐ *ze*   to nationalize

☐ *tn*   nationalisation

☐ *o*   national (noun), citizen

The arrow

The arrow is the most versatile and arguably the most useful of all the symbols. You can do pretty much anything with arrows and below is a very limited selection.

←	return, come back, reverse, regress
↗	rise, increase, grow, climb etc.
↘	fall, decline, slide, slip, drop, shrink,
⇔	exchange, relations,
→	lead to, consequence of, therefore
↪	continue,
↩	…

The last two can mean many things. What is important is that, if you use them, that meaning is clear to you.

The arrow is the ultimate distillation of meaning. It can be used to note many different things and as such it leaves interpreters with more freedom to choose the vocabulary of their version than any other symbol. This was demonstrated by Rozan as follows (2003:29 [1956:32])

country's ↗	= a country's development
↗ duties	= an increase in duties
↗ science	= scientific progress
↗ patient	= the patient's recovery
↗ salaries	= a rise in salaries
↗ living st^{ard}	= an improvement in the standard of living
↗ prices	= inflation

People

My own personal favourite amongst symbols is based on the circle, representing a head, and by extension meaning "person". This gives us two sets of symbols, firstly for human emotion and thought.

☺	pleased. (You don't need to, and shouldn't, draw the eyes in the circle... this type face however insists.)
☹	annoyed, unhappy, unimpressed, etc.
☹	very unhappy, disgusted, etc
Õ	to think
Ō	to know, (for me, the straight line denotes certainty, in comparison to the squiggly line for "to think".)

You can easily create more of your own symbols along these lines if need be. Imagine, for example, a symbol for "shocked, surprised".

The circle can also be used to denote a person who is associated with that symbol's meaning. This can be done by adding a raised circle to another symbol.

☐ al	national (adjective)	☐ o	national (noun), citizen
econ	Economy	econ o	economist
E	Energy	E o	energy expert, supplier,
π	Policy	π o	politician
∩	that, which	∩o	who

Underlining

Underlining, and the different ways we can underline, belong to this category of organic symbols. If in our notes we want to show that something is <u>important</u> or even more <u>important</u> it is quicker to underline it than write out more words. It is also useful for degrees of a quality: thus *large, huge, colossal* might be notes as *big,* *big,* and *big,* respectively. Similarly if something is less clear-cut we can show this through broken underlining. It is a very useful of technique and can give us a whole new wealth of concepts from a symbol or word we have noted. Let's take a few from the lists above.

↗	rise (etc.)
↗ (underlined)	rise sharply, jump, soar,
↗ (double underlined)	rise dramatically, leap, skyrocket etc
↗ (dashed underline)	faltering rise, etc

You can of course underline anything, words included. So *say* becomes *assert* and *poor* becomes *destitute*.

say	assert,
poor	very poor
poor	grinding, crushing poverty, destitution,
poor	fairly poor, more or less badly off,

For a further example of organic symbol construction see the section on Verbs (page 133) in Part II.

Where to find symbols

The symbols you use should have some element of mnemonic, that is they should mean something to you by association (for example my chimney stack on page 102). They should create associations in YOUR mind. This means that copying other people's symbols is not always a good idea. However, symbols can be very useful and there are already lots of them around, so don't reinvent the wheel! Use the symbols you know and "organify" them.

Look at the very incomplete list of examples below. I will not suggest any "meaning" for the symbols, but if you immediately recognize a symbol or associate it with a concept then that will be a good symbol for you to use. The rest you can (and will) forget.

Mathematics	$\pm$ $\neq$ π $\%$ $>$ $<$ $=$ $\therefore$
Science	Σ σ Δ E t $\propto$
Music	$\#$ ♫ $\angle$

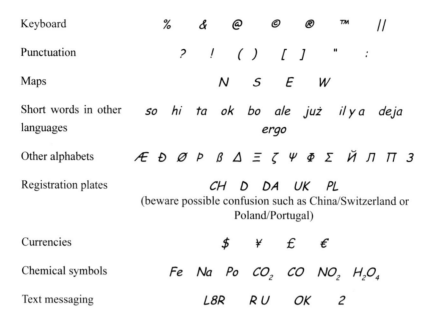

| Keyboard | % | & | @ | © | ® | ™ | // |

| Punctuation | ? | ! | ( ) | [ ] | " | : |

| Maps | N | S | E | W |

| Short words in other languages | so hi ta ok bo ale już il y a deja ergo |

| Other alphabets | Æ Đ Ø Þ ß Δ Ξ ζ Ψ Φ Σ Й Л П З |

| Registration plates | CH D DA UK PL |
(beware possible confusion such as China/Switzerland or Poland/Portugal)

| Currencies | $ ¥ £ € |

| Chemical symbols | Fe Na Po CO_2 CO NO_2 H_2O_4 |

| Text messaging | L8R R U OK 2 |

How to practise

1. Go through the transcripts of speeches you have worked with in this book or from elsewhere and see which concepts (synonymous words and expressions) come up most often. Make a list and think up or borrow a symbol for the most common ones.

2. Go through the consecutive notepads you have been using so far. Ask yourself, "which long words am I writing out repeatedly?" Can you think up a quick and simple symbol to replace them?

3. Go through your consecutive note pads. Which words are you sometimes noting as symbols, sometimes not? Cross out the words where you have used them and replace them with the symbols you have chosen. (This exercise is not about "correcting" the notes, you may never even look at the set of notes again, but the action of crossing something out and replacing it will help anchor that symbol in your memory.) It is important to use symbols consistently and automatically.

Finally, don't worry too much about symbols. There is no right or wrong amount of symbols to use, but sticking to the rules outlined at the beginning of the chapter will make sure that, however many or few you use, they help rather than hinder. In the short term you will try out lots of symbols but in the long run symbols will pretty much choose themselves. The ones that get used, those that represent the most common concepts in speeches, will get remembered and the ones that don't get used will be forgotten. And so it should it be.

Chapter 7   Memory Prompts

The note-taking system described in Chapters 1-6 is simple and consistent, but the notes you are now taking are too complete, something you may have noticed when practising (because you can't write fast enough). In this chapter you will find a few suggestions on how to reduce the amount of notes you take, in some cases radically, and let your memory take over. Notes are there to help your memory, not replace it.

You have already seen a number of simple techniques for taking fewer notes.

Not noting the verb *to be* **or** *there is/are.*

Noting the speaker as *We* **or** *I* **rather than in full, as you will know who the speaker represents.**

Not noting *We* **or** *I* **if it is clear the speaker is the subject of the sentence.**

The recall line[§]**.** Another simple technique for noting less. It is explained in Part II, Recall Line (page 135).

Each of these cases is a mechanical reduction and there is not much to remember. In this chapter we will see that the memory can do much more than this if it is given the right prompts. If you think back to Chapter 3 (page 52), you will remember that we saw that despite incomplete notes we were able to recall a lot of information from our notes. Below we expand on this technique.

Structure can help recall information

The very presence of an structural element in your notes may remind you of all the information to which it referred.

Brackets   *(   )*

In Chapter 5 we saw how information of secondary importance could be noted in brackets below the element in your notes to which it belonged. Here we go one step further and note only an empty pair of brackets, or a pair of brackets with a single word in them. This will be enough to jog our memory and recall what information was contained in them in the original.

We've seen the example below (**MacShane 1**) before in Chapter 5. Have a look at the same notes below, but from which I have now removed information from the brackets. Aren't these notes still enough to jog your memory, even now, 10 pages later? Check against the full text below.

changes	
( )	
	remarkable
	_____
Europe 1973	
( )	
	gone
	_____

currencies +	
curr controls	
(block	
fair	
transp ^{t} bus ^{ns})	
effec ^{v}	
replace/	
	by single market
	( )
	_____

Here I have only left three of four sets of brackets "empty", but depending on your own recall powers you could have left any number of them "empty" when you took your notes. If this seems a little daunting at first try noting a single word in the brackets to represent a larger chunk of information. In the example above this would give you *(UK)*, *(borders)* and *(euro)* respectively. Again this is something that you will work out for yourself as you gain in experience and get you know your own capabilities. Two people will not necessarily be able to recall the same things.

Compare what you can remember with the full text below. (**MacShane 1**)

> And today? The changes, even since 1973, when Britain entered the European Economic Community, are remarkable:
> The Europe of 1973 with its border control on goods and cars has gone. The myriad of currencies and currency controls acting as a blockage to fair, transparent, effective business has been replaced by a single market. One where the majority of EU citizens sensibly use one currency - the Euro.

When you practise, don't be afraid of trying out this technique and not being able to recall the information in the brackets. Failing and trying again is an important part of the learning process. It is important to explore your own limits and capabilities through frequent practice so that when you come to do it for real you know exactly to what extent you can rely on your memory. That is all part of testing yourself, knowing your limits and stretching them.

Examples *eg*

Often just noting *eg...* or *eg* plus one word will be enough to remind us of an entire example because the context and the illustrative nature of the example will make it easier to recall. To save time don't note the full stops in the grammatically correct *e.g.* .

Example

In the example below, (henceforth **MacShane 2**) the speaker, Denis MacShane, the UK Minister for Europe, is in Romania talking about accession to the EU and problems that Romania faces. The speech was delivered on 7th October 2003, and is available at the URL given on page 228.

> Linked to tackling corruption, Romania needs also further to demonstrate its commitment to reform in the judicial and law enforcement field. Successfully tackling drug smuggling and organised crime requires more resources and training for judges and police and better cooperation between law enforcement authorities. These are real challenges. But you can count on the UK and other EU partners to help you with them, provided the political commitment and direction is there.
> **I'd like to give you an example. Yesterday I attended a reception linked to a successful UK/Romanian project called Project Reflex. This aimed to tackle human trafficking and illegal immigration: pitiful enterprises trading in human misery and exploitation across borders. The project has been a success because of the efforts on both sides.** A combination of criminal intelligence specialists and equipment from the UK, and experienced

and dedicated Romanian police with local knowledge.

Your notes might look like this:

```
┌──────────────┬────────────────────────────────────────────┐
│              │  You                                        │
│              │                                             │
│              │                         can count on        │
│              │                                  UK          │
│              │                                  EU          │
│              │                                             │
│              │                                             │
│  if          │  political will                             │
│              │                    _____             │
│              │                                             │
│              │                                             │
│  eg          │                                             │
│              │  REFLEX ...                                 │
└──────────────┴────────────────────────────────────────────┘
```

This is all we need to note for the passage up to the words *efforts on both sides*. Why? Well, look at the context: the speaker has given us fair warning that he is going to give an example of a success, so we needn't note that; it will be obvious. We can remember it was at a function yesterday, but even if we don't, it is not the most important part of the passage. Next, we're in Romania and the speaker has been talking about policing, so the number one topic will usually be immigration and human trafficking, and we remember that this is a very harrowing phenomenon. And finally, the speaker has also been talking about cooperation, so this example will surely be a result of it. Et *voilà*, you have all the information to reproduce the original, but you only noted *eg REFLEX*. (NB The capital letters indicate that this is a proper name and therefore we won't confuse it with "reflex". See Part II, How you write it, page 161.)

Finally, you will remember all of this, not because your memory is exceptional, nor because you noted it in extenso (quite the contrary), but because your limited but structured notes helped your memory do its job, by allowing you to listen more intently (because you're not writing) and by providing the right prompts.

Reasons   *cos*

Noting *cos*, representing "because of", and the indication that something must be recalled (three dots ...) is enough to remind us of what we didn't note.

Example (**Patten**)

> On Chechnya, there have, it is true, been some recent moderately positive developments in response to international and European Union pressure:

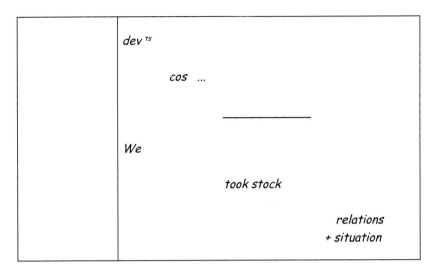

A clear prompt like this will help our intelligence, knowledge or memory do the rest. Here the missing information was *in response to international and EU pressure.*

The same technique works with other words, like *but*, for example, which could also be enough to prompt the recall of a whole argument. See below, Opposites.

Opposites - two sides of an argument

Often if a speaker is describing two differing standpoints it will be unnecessary to note the second half of the argument. Instead we can reproduce it because we know that it is the opposite of the first half (which we noted) or because we know it from own general knowledge.

Example (**MacShane 1**)

> The Europe of 1973 with dirty beaches, and expensive air travel and telephone calls has been replaced by a Europe which allows more people to travel, talk to each other and enjoy a shared and better-protected natural environment than ever before.

In this example we need not note *a Europe which allows more people to travel, talk to each other and enjoy a shared and better-protected natural environment than ever before* as it is basically the exact opposite of *dirty beaches, and expensive air travel and telephone calls.* All we need is a marker in our notes to tell us that. Here I have used *by...* but we could equally have used a pair of empty brackets to show that something has not been noted (see also above Brackets).

Europe 1973

    (*dirty*   *beaches*
        expen ᵛ   *air*
              phone   )

              replaced

                        by...

---

    by... shows clearly that something is missing in the notes and, knowing that this technique is part of our note-taking system, we will assume that it is the opposite of *dirty beaches, and expensive air travel and telephone calls.* (You will note that the speaker has merely reversed their order for stylistic reasons). Again leaving things out like this will be a very personal affair and you must experiment for yourselves. Much will depend on your own general knowledge, understanding of the subject matter and context of any given speech. The only way to find out what works for you is to practise these techniques and see when they work and when they don't.

> In the examples in the sections Examples, Reasons and Opposites above I have used three dots ... to show where a gap in the notes has to be filled from memory. You could equally a pair of empty brackets if that works better for you.

How to practise – structure can help recall information

1. Go through the texts of speeches you have worked with in this book or from elsewhere and see where you might have applied the techniques described above.

2. Practise taking notes from transcripts and the spoken word and deliberately "leaving things out" of your notes in the ways described above. Go back through the notes afterwards and see what you can remember of what you didn't note.

It will take a lot of practice before you get to know how your memory works and what is effective for you. So do a lot of it!

Things right in front of you

Often you will be called upon to interpret consecutively when travelling with a group. You may be visiting an industrial installation with a delegation of business men when the host decides to explain what everything is and does; your group may be having a guided tour of a local tourist spot as part of their social and cultural programme. But what you will often find is that the machinery, building, landscape or whatever being talked about by the speaker, which is right in front of you to see and behold, can be used as a large mental notepad, or as we described it in Chapter 1, a three-dimensional mind map. If the speaker starts their explanation, say, at the top of the machine and works down through the process it runs; or from the bottom of a building upwards describing how it was built and the events accompanying the construction; or from the West of a landscape to the East; you have a huge 3-D colour notepad already laid out before you with a perfect set of notes telling you what comes first, second and third. In such cases you would be well advised to look and listen, and not to note. You will be amazed at how easily it all comes back to you.

Note the simple for the complicated

Speakers tend to be flowery in their presentations, or use a higher register than we are used to. This can sometimes tempt us into trying to include descriptive detail or specific words in our notes when it isn't really necessary. If you note a simplified version of the original you will remember that the speaker was more eloquent or fulsome in their delivery and adjust appropriately. In the example below the second sentence is long, and full of long words, but really all that is being said, in telegraphic form, is *climate change means more weird weather*. You should note the minimum, and let your memory recall the details when you interpret. In the example below you don't want to get caught trying to note things like *weather event*, you will remember that the speaker used a rather convoluted register for this passage and adjust appropriately.

***Example* (Hodgson)**

> But what I will tell you – and what a climatologist would tell you – is that this is what climate change looks like. One of the significant consequences expected from climate change is an increase in the frequency and severity of extreme weather events.

B

I

       will say

∩ climate change

         = similar
         _____

//   *1 result*

        =

            more storms
            _____

→   *...*

In this example the information *is an increase in the frequency and severity of extreme weather events.* is noted in minimalist form. The notation **more storms** does not give us all the information we need, however it does give us the prompt our memory needs to dig up that information, information about register and detail.

Stories and jokes

One word, symbol or even little picture can be enough to recall the whole story or joke.

Example (**MacShane 2**)

> A few weeks ago, I was asked whether I would like to give a speech to a Romanian audience on the big European issue of the day. I agreed wholeheartedly. Where better to test my theories on Romanian superstar Adrian Mutu's effect on Chelsea's chances in the European Cup, I thought. Then my Private Secretary told me they meant they wanted me to talk about the Inter-Governmental Conference (IGC).

If you followed English football in 2003/4 the final two sentences of this paragraph (indeed the whole paragraph if you haven't already started taking notes) could comfortably be noted as *MUTU*.

Or your notes might look like this,

	I
	was asked
to speak	
	on Eur issue
	to ROM °
	_____
I	
	agreed
	_____
MUTU !	

This way of not noting things, or just noting the key word will always depend to a large extent on you, your mind, what you know and the context. It will work best in subject areas that you are familiar with and understand. I offer this as an example of how it can work, not as an suggestion that you should have noted this particular example in the same way. Again I encourage you to practise a lot and to test and explore your own limits.

In this paragraph the "joke" that he is not supposed to talk about Adrian Mutu but the IGC is not hard to remember. Now you may say, "but what about all the details? *Adrian (Mutu's first name), Chelsea, European Cup, Private Secretary, IGC. „*.

There are two things to say about the details of any joke:
1. They are not as important as the joke itself! And if you don't get the joke then the details are lost anyway. You might say:

> A great opportunity to show what I know about Romanian superstar Adrian Mutu's effect on English football, I thought. Then one of my staff told me I was supposed to talk about the IGC.

2. And will anyone worry? They are not the same words but it is the same joke.

If you do know about football, (and the standard titles for Ministry staff in the UK), all the detail (*Adrian (Mutu's first name), Chelsea, European Cup, Private Secretary, IGC*) will come from your general knowledge NOT from your notes. Which brings us nicely on the next point...

It depends on what you already know

General knowledge is a great substitute for notes. If you know something, you remember it. It is just there in your mind. This means that any similar events or explanations need not be noted in full as most of the information is already available to you from your own general knowledge. Look at the example below.

Example (MacShane 1)

> Let me explain. In 1980 and 1981 I was heavily involved in supporting the independent Polish Union, Solidarność. In 1982 I was arrested and imprisoned in Warsaw when taking money to the underground activists of the union – men and women who today occupy high places in the national life of Poland.
>
> When I was released I was declared persona non grata by the communist government. I could not get a visa for Poland. My friends struggling for Polish freedom could not travel to the West. But we could both travel visa free to Varna. So on the sands of the Black Sea, the contacts were re-established, and over a glass of the wonderful wine that Bulgaria has the genius to produce, my footnote in the history of Europe's liberation from communism continued to be written.

This little story about Poland might seem rather unusual coming from a British Minister speaking in Bulgaria. But if you are familiar with the events of the 1980s in Poland the whole passage could be noted simply as,

'82 Warsaw → Varna

It would be immediately apparent to someone familiar with modern Polish history what the chain of events was. Your train of thought, when you see *Warsaw* in your notes might run something like this....

> Warsaw, what happened in Warsaw? Arrested, why? Taking money to the underground activists. NB those same people are now prominent politicians. So arrested, therefore no visa. In 1981/2, Poles, we know, can't leave the country. Therefore they had to meet in Varna, and that's how I know Varna. What's in Varna? Good wine and beaches.... and that is my part in history.

How to practise

1. When listening to speeches that you are going to interpret consecutively make a deliberate effort to identify parts of the speech that could be easily recalled through minimal notes - for example the type of thing mentioned in this chapter. Force yourself NOT to note as fully as you would like but to use one of the techniques above. Not everything will work for you all the time, but it is important to work out what you yourself are capable of through a process of trial and error.

2. Take a set of notes you have just produced. Go through them and decide which bits of the notes could you have done without. In a separate notepad try to create a shorter version from which you would still be able to reproduce the original speech. This is exercise is called telescoping (Rozan, 2003:49 [1956:58]).
After the speech, and under no time pressure you will find there are many "improvements" that you can make to your notes. Regularly doing this exercise will help you to note more succinctly while listening in the future.

3. While listening to a speech take notes as per usual. At the end of the speech put your notes to one side and try to reproduce the speech from memory (Seleskovitch and Lederer, 2002:59). This is quite a daunting exercise, but it will demonstrate the degree to which note-taking distracts us from the task of listening. To do this well you need to have a clear picture of the structure of the speech in your mind. This can be the same structure you committed to the notepad, but you will have to arrive at it without the help of your notes.

Chapter 8   What to Note

Up until now I have been encouraging a very limited approach to note-taking. Because we are new to consecutive interpreting, we have concentrated on the basic structures in our notes and the analysis of the speech we are listening too. As you master the techniques described so far you can start to take more care about the details; something you will continue doing later on in your careers.

Once the basics, the ideas and the links, which we have already spent some time on, are on paper (points 1- 4 below), the list focuses on things that are not easily remembered but which are often very important. This chapter is, if you like, the opposite of the previous one, where we saw what things don't need to be noted because they were easy to remember. Here are a few things you won't want to forget but which are harder to recall.

1.   Ideas

2.   Links

The reasons and methods for noting these elements are discussed in detail in Chapter 4.

3.   Who is speaking

It is crucial for the listener to know who is speaking, whose point of view is being represented. It is also very useful for the interpreter to repeatedly remind themselves who they are speaking for in order to help get the right tone, register and lexis for that speech. (See Part II, Margins, page 137).

4.   Verb tense and modal verbs

Tenses and modal verbs will always be crucial to the semantics of the speech and as such you should have a clear system for noting them. (See Part II, Verbs, page 132).

5.   Proper names, Numbers, Dates, Lists

These four belong to the same category of elements. They are not integral to the grammar of the sentence nor the causality of the ideas and are therefore very difficult to remember without notes. It is a good idea to note them immediately, interrupting whatever you are noting to note the number, date, proper name or list and then return to where you left off. This is because, often, they cannot be remembered from context and noted later as ideas can. See Part II Noting sooner, or later.

Names - if you don't know a name, note it phonetically and see if you can work out how to say it properly in your target language later. If you can't, then substitute a generic like "the UK delegate" rather than mangling the name.
Lists should be noted vertically, as in Chapter 5.

6.   Terms to be transcoded[§]

Sometimes a speaker will use certain words, often technical terminology, very deliberately, and these must be repeated, not processed and paraphrased in the target language.

7.   The last sentence of a speech

Often the last sentence, or few sentences, of a speech will contain an important message, perhaps a jokey remark, or a motto summing up the whole speech. And often the speaker will announce that they are wrapping up. Many interpreters will listen with extra care to this part of the speech, then abandon their usual minimalist approach to note-taking and note it in some detail. This is possible because the speaker will stop talking at some stage and with no more incoming source speech you can devote your mental resources to remembering what was said and how to note it.

These pointers have been compiled and summarized from books you will find in the bibliography at the back.

PART II

Fine-tuning

1. Clauses

In Chapter 2 we looked at the Subject Verb Object group as the basic model for communicating ideas. We concentrated on the Object, (according to our generous definition of it,) as the third element of the idea in order not to over-complicate the initial stages of our introduction to note-taking for consecutive. Very often though the third (or fourth) element of the group is not just a single noun but a whole clause. Let's look at two common types of clauses.

The first type of clause often follows verbs of speech or thought, like, "say", "think", "declare", "consider" and as such makes regular appearances in the types of speech we want to interpret. In the extracts below the clauses are marked in bold.

S   V

...our basic message is **that a sound programme will be vital to boost investor confidence**. **(Patten)**

S   V

last week the Prime Minister said **[that] the government was doing all it could**... **(Blair 1)**

S   V

A study done for the Ministry for the Environment said **[that] a southward shift in subtropical pasture species might be one indicator** **(Hodgson)**

Clauses obey the same rules of grammar as our idea groups and you will notice that in the examples of clauses above the clause itself, like the first part of the sentence it is contained in, has a Subject, a Verb and sometimes an Object.

s   v   o

...that a sound programme will be vital to boost investor confidence. (Patten)

s   v   o

... (that) the government was doing all it could... (Blair 1)

s   v   o

a southward shift in subtropical pasture species might be one indicator (Hodgson)

This then leads us to the simplest way of dealing with this structure - an extension of the technique we use for the standard SVO group. First we take a symbol which denotes "clause" and we note it at the left of the page. (Exactly how far left you place the symbol will depend on your reaction to Chapter 5, Shifting values.)

The following symbol can be used to represent the word *that* and to introduce clauses. It is quick, simple and clear.

∩   = *that, which*

Then we note the SVO group in the clause from left to right as usual. The examples above would be noted,

Example 1

...our basic message is **that a sound programme will be vital to boost investor confidence. (Patten)**

	message
	=
	∩
	sound prog
	$\underline{\text{imp}}^{t}$
	↗ *inv* ° *confid*
	————

Notice that this technique also has the distinct practical advantage of creating more space on the notepad page. We cannot continue off to the right-hand side indefinitely!

Example 2

last week the Prime Minister said **[that] the government was doing all it could**... **(Blair 1)**

	PM
	" ⌐
	n
	govt
	doing
	utmost
	⎯⎯⎯⎯⎯

Example 3

A study done for the Ministry for the Environment said [**that**]**a southward shift in subtropical pasture species might be one indicator** (Hodgson)

//	Study (Min Env) " ⌐
	n
	↓ S /subtrop past ʳ species
	=
	indicator
	⎯⎯⎯⎯⎯

A second type of clause adds information to the third part of our Subject Verb Object unit. These clauses are usually preceded in English by words like, "that", "which", "who", although not always. In the extracts below this type clause is marked in bold.

> Since then there have been a number of significant events **that may affect our path to the European Union**, for example the Summit in Helsinki. **(Buzek)**

> At WSSD we made important commitments on energy **that will help us tackle climate change. (Whitty)**

Using the same symbol to mark the start of the clause we can solve this problem.

∩	*that, which, what*, etc. including indirect speech. NB The word "*that*" is often implicit in English (and in some other languages); make it explicit in your notes. Also *where, when, who* are used to introduce subordinate clauses.
∩°	who, whose, whom (the ° denotes a person)

Example 1 (Buzek)

> Since then there have been a number of significant events that may affect our path to the European Union, for example the Summit in Helsinki.

since	*events*
	∩
	may affect
	path to EU
	(eg Helsinki)

This structure avoids any confusion that might have led us to say things like, *since then a number of events may affect our path.....* or *since then a number of events have affected our path.....*

Example 2

In this example (henceforth **Whitty**) Lord Whitty of Camberwell, Minister for Farming, Food and Sustainable Energy, is speaking at the 5th British-German Environment Forum in Berlin, on 5th February 2004. The Germans, remember, are much greener than the British. The full text is available at the URL given on page 229.

> At WSSD we made important commitments on energy that will help us tackle climate change.

We
(At WSSD)
            made
                        imp⁺ commitments

∩

            ⌐help   tackle
                        climate change
            _____

These are of course very straightforward examples, in reality you will have recognize such clauses from much longer and more complex sentences as well. What's important to remember, though, is that the clause is not as important as the major part of the sentence (and that's why some of these clauses are called subordinate clauses).

There also is a certain overlap here with the type of thing we noted in brackets in Chapter 5 (page 92), and it will be for you to decide when you turn to brackets and when you use this technique. As a rule of thumb, this technique works for longer, more detailed additions, whereas the brackets are better for things that can be recalled from single words or symbols in our notes.

2. Rules of Abbreviation

Don't write out long words in full in your consecutive notes, you don't have time. Take the first few letters of the word and some part of the end of the word, raised. The following brief extract says it all.

The rule of thumb is that unless a word is short (4-5 letters) the interpreter should note it in an abbreviated form.

If we have to note "specialized" it is more meaningful and reliable to note sp^{ed} than to write *spec*.

Other examples:

Stat. could be read as "statute" or "statistics" whilst St^{ute} and St^{ics} are unambiguous.

Prod. could be read as "production", "producer", "product" or "productivity" while Pr^{on}, Pr^{er}, Pr^{ct}, Pr^{vity} are unambiguous.

Com. could be read as "Commission" or "committee" while C^{on} and C^{tee} are unambiguous.

Rozan, 2003:11 [1956:9]

In every language there are suffixes which many different words share. Some English examples are noted below. Many of these will also apply to the Romance languages. If you are noting in German or Polish then some abbreviation for the common endings "-ung" and "-owość" might be a good idea.

Abstractions

Suffix	Note	Example	
-ition		constitution	$const^{n}$
-ation		institution	$inst^{n}$
-ution	n	production	$prod^{n}$
-ision			
		re-nationalize	$renat^{z}$
-ize, -ise	z	privatize	$priv^{z}$
		monopolize	$monop^{z}$

-itive		executive	*exec* [v]
-isive	*v*	comprehensive	*comp* [v]
-ative		inclusive	*incl* [v]
-ivity	*y*	productivity	*prod*[y]
		competitivity	*comp*[y]
		exclusivity	*exclu*[y]
-ment	*t*	government	*gov*[t]
		development	*dev* [t]
-able	*b*	fashionable	*fash* [b]
		biodegradable	*biodegrad* [b]

If these abbreviations don't correspond to your language, use the same technique to create some that do.

Phonetic spelling and misspelling

Another way of abbreviating is to spell words phonetically rather than correctly. See How you write it, page 161, for more.

3. Verbs

Verb conjugations

The point of departure is the infinitive form of the verb, an abbreviation of it, or a symbol representing it. Do not get into the habit of noting in full conjugations, auxiliary verbs, endings etc. The conjugation will be clear because you will know what the subject is that goes with the verb, so English speakers have no need to write *works* for *he works* where *work* is quicker. It is inconceivable that you will make a grammatical mistake because of your abbreviated notes and say **he work* when you interpret.

Similarly it is a complete waste of time to note *he doesn't work* when *X work* is shorter and more obvious on the page.

Questions should not be noted with the reversed word order they have in most languages, *Does he know the consequences?* but in the affirmative order with a question mark at the beginning of the sentence and the infinitive (or a symbol for it). *? Know consequences?*. See also the section on Questions in Part II, Uses of the Margin on page 137.

he works	*work*
he doesn't work	*X work*
Does he know the consequences	*? know consequences?*

You may think that these few letters fewer will make little difference, but repeated a dozen times in the course of one speech, as such constructions will be, you will save valuable time.

Verb tenses

Verb tenses come up all the time and the differences between them are often fundamental to understanding the speech. You will need a technique for noting these differences. Below is a simple method for doing so.

work	to work
work ^{9}	working
work/	worked
/work	will work

wôrk	would work
wôrk/	would have worked

Of course the system if valid with any other verb.

Example (**MacShane 1**)

I am delighted to be back here in Sofia. The first time I came to Bulgaria was 20 years ago and then I never dreamed I would return as a UK government minister. Let me explain. In 1980 and 1981 I was heavily involved in supporting the independent Polish Union, Solidarność. In 1982 I was arrested and imprisoned in Warsaw when taking money to the underground activists of the union – men and women who today occupy high places in the national life of Poland.

	Let me explain	
	_____	
I		
	involve /	
		Solidarnosc
		( )
	_____	
1982		
	arrest /	
	imprison /	
		( )
	_____	

Modal verbs

Like verb tenses, modal verbs are crucial to the message a speaker is trying to convey. They also crop up regularly and can be quite long words to write in full, certainly in some languages, you don't want to be writing words like, *pourraient, should, powinien, moechten,* every 2 minutes, to take examples from French,

English, Polish and German respectively. Some modal verbs, *can, may, must, need,* etc. are already very short and we won't need a symbol or abbreviation for them. Below I suggest some examples for English; if your mother tongue is not English, you can use the English verbs as a form of abbreviation. Beware though, as the range of meaning of each modal verb is often different from one language to another. If you don't note in English, or if the suggestions below don't "click" for you, then just come up with your own symbols and abbreviations.

should	*shd*	must	>
could	*cd*	may	*may*
would	^		

4. The Recall Line

You should not note the same word or symbol twice on the same page. It is almost always quicker to draw a line from where that word, symbol or construction first appears to where is appears the second time. Some interpreters like to underline whatever is being repeated in order to be doubly clear. This is a matter of personal taste. Don't use the recall line for links. We want them to remain very clear on the page. Two pointers:

1. Make sure that you use a simple line, when you wish to show that the same thing is repeated in a second section of your notes AND NOT a line with an arrow at the end, which may wrongly suggest a causal relationship between two parts of the speech that is not intended. THE RECALL LINE IS NOT A LINK, it is a quick mechanical way of avoiding noting the same thing twice on one page.
2. It is important when drawing a recall line not to obscure notes that you have already written. The recall line does not need to be straight, and so as far as possible you should avoid passing through words and symbols already on the page so as not to render them illegible (See Figure 5 below).

Example (**Blair 2**)

First, any successful economy needs to conform to certain basics. It should be an open economy, willing to let capital and goods move freely. It needs financial and monetary discipline - the markets and investors swiftly punish the profligate. It needs to encourage business and enterprise - to create an enabling climate for entrepreneurs.

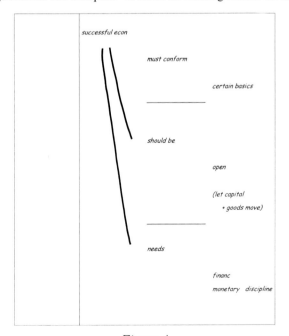

Figure 4

In the continuation of the same passage the recall line even passes over to the next page, but this does not cause the interpreter any problem because they are the third and fourth in a series of lines emanating from the same word. If you are using the page-turning technique described in the section Moving On…(page 73), you will see that the two parts of the line join up across the two pages. You can use recall lines across pages even when the first line crosses from one page to another, but you should be careful not to waste time doing it, nor run the risk of not being sure of what it refers back to. As with all these tricks, its only purpose is to help. If it doesn't, don't use it.

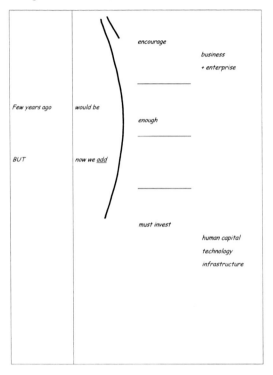

Figure 5

5.   Uses of the Margin

In Chapter 4 we noted links (and the all important "no link") in the margin on the left hand side because of their importance within the speech and because it fitted in with our left-to-right notation of the Subject Verb Object group from Chapter 3. In this section we will see that there are other important elements of a speech that can also be noted in the left-hand margin in order to make them stand out, and thus facilitate the production stage of consecutive.

These elements may be split into four categories:

1. Opinions
2. Structural elements - numbering, digressions and questions
3. Dates
4. Anything important!

Opinions

If we feel that who is expressing some opinion is particularly important, we can highlight it by noting it in the margin on the left of the page. This follows on from Chapter 5, Shifting Values.

Example (**Torry 1**)

I was looking recently at a survey of young people's attitudes in both countries.

Germans see the UK as a good place to work and to study - second only to the US. They recognise that we have a creative, multicultural society. But Germans see us as reluctant Europeans. They have the impression that we don't like them very much.

Young British people said they admired Germany's high-quality cars and its well-organised people. But they still associated Germany with the 12 years between 1933 and 1945.

```
Ger °
           think

           ∩

           UK
                         = good to   work

                                 study
                                 (    )

                         _____
```

```
UK °

           think

           ∩
```

Structural elements

Numbering

Some speakers will break what they have to say up into chunks and number them: "firstly", "secondly" etc. Some will lose count as they pass three and others will mention no numbers at all. Whatever the speaker might do, the interpreter will be well served by noting numbers in the left hand margin. This will remind you, even three or four pages later in the notepad, that indeed the ideas belong in some broader structure (a list) within the speech as a whole. This will help you to follow the thrust of the argument the speaker is making and to give the correct intonation to each part of the speech when you speak.

In the example below (**Patten**), the speaker has been kind enough to mention the numbers and even to do so correctly, even though each of his numbered ideas are several seconds and sentences apart. The interpreter should return the favour by noting clearly in the margin the same numbers as in the example below.

Example

The European Council on 19th and 20th June was a very valuable meeting of important consolidation. The agenda was very broad and I simply want to focus on what seemed to the Commission to be some of the most important highlights. **First** the heads of state and government confirmed that Greece meets the necessary conditions to enter the third phase of economic and monetary union. Greece will join the euro zone from 1st January next year which I hope will send messages to one or two other countries, including the one I know best.

Second, the European Council took stock of the progress made in implementing the economic and social agenda adopted at Lisbon. The Council gave, as the Prime Minister said, renewed encouragement to the work that has already been begun, particularly on the e-Europe action plan, research and enterprise policy and the extremely important subject of social inclusion.

In September the Commission will submit its proposals for indicators that will allow us to measure how well we are performing in meeting the goals set at Lisbon. These indicators can then be used as the basis for the synthesis report to the European Council in spring next year.

Thirdly, some progress was achieved on completing the internal market. In particular Europe's energy markets are to be further liberalised and air transport will be made more efficient by creating what has come to be called a single European sky.

Fourth, the Council welcomed the broad economic guidelines for 2000 and recommended their adoption by the Council. These guidelines reflect the need to sustain growth and to continue pursuing macro-economic policies that promote stability. The guidelines lay particular emphasis on the quality and sustainability of public finances and the need to continue reforming Europe's product, capital and labour markets. The Council restated its commitment to carrying through reforms that are essential to enable Europe to become a truly knowledge-based economy.

Each new number reminds us of the wider context. However long a particular point, it is still only one of a list of points of more or less equal importance, even if they are noted several pages apart in our notes.

Digressions ( )

It is important not only to identify a digression (which by definition will be of secondary importance) when you hear it, but also when you come back to it as you reproduce the speech from your notes, so that you can adjust your tone and speed of delivery appropriately - digressions are usually delivered more quickly and at a lower volume, in accordance with their secondary status within the speech. This can be done very simply by prefacing a digression or aside with an "open bracket" (in the margin and closing the aside with a "close bracket"), also in the left hand margin.

Example

This example (henceforth **Reid**) is taken from a speech by John Reid MP, Secretary of State for Health in the UK, 28th April 2004. The title of the speech is 'Choosing health - closing the gap on inequalities'. Mr Reid is talking to health professionals from the National Health Service (NHS) about reforms to the service aimed at ensuring equal access to health services for all.

> At a conference about inequalities I want to start with the founding principles that set up the NHS. Our health system is based upon the principle of equal access to health care, free at the point of need. It is paid for out of general taxation and to date I have seen no evidence that there is a better way of providing equity of access for an entire nation.
> It won't come as a surprise to you, incidentally, and this is an aside, that is largely why I am opposed to the so called Patient's Passport, a policy that will undermine that basic principle of equity. You cannot maintain an NHS that provides equal access for all if you subsidise those people who can pay to jump the queue above those who cannot. And you cannot give everyone the same chance of surviving ill health if you subsidise those people that can pay to jump the queue over those that cannot.
> But while I want to do nothing to move backwards, away from the principle of equity, I do not want to pretend either, that we have constructed a system that achieves it perfectly in practice.

The entire second paragraph is a digression, so we might note it as follows:

The passage and your notes continue for sometime, until we get to:

if	
	subsidize
	rich queue jumpers
)	not poor
	_____

Notice that I have put the close bracket in the margin at the left and not on the right of the page. It is much more visible there.

Questions

It is better to know before you start talking that what you are going to say is a question. It makes a great difference to how you say it! To do this, we borrow a Spanish idea of putting the question mark at the beginning (and, if you like, also the end) of the question. This simple trick also gets around the unnecessary trouble of changing the word order from SVO in our questions.

Example (Torry 1)

> The big question that everyone is asking at the moment is about Europe's relationship with the US. Should Europe try to build itself up as a kind of counterweight to the United States? Or should we try to work in partnership with them?

```
┌──────────────┬─────────────────────────────────────┐
│              │                                     │
│              │  Question                           │
│              │  ( about EU - US )                  │
│              │                                     │
│              │                      =              │
│              │                                     │
│   ¿          │  counterweight ?                    │
│              │                                     │
│   or         │                                     │
│              │                                     │
│   ¿          │  partnership ?                      │
│              │                                     │
│              │                   _____     │
│              │                                     │
└──────────────┴─────────────────────────────────────┘
```

By the same token, note the question word (*why, how, who, where, when, what*), preceded by a question mark in the margin at the left. Often as in the example below the question leads to an answer...what the speaker wants to say... and each question in a series begins a new section of the speaker's train of thought. It will be easier to give the question the correct intonation when you reproduce the speech if the question is clearly visible on the page of your notes in advance.

Example (**Torry 1**)

So how are we to meet this challenge?

In a globalised world, Europe needs to modernise and reform if it is to remain competitive. It was for this reason that the Heads of State and Government of the European Union agreed in Lisbon in 2000 a series of ambitious goals. The aim was to make Europe the world's most competitive economy by 2010.

So what do we need to do to achieve this?

First, we need to liberalise our markets and to make them more flexible. Take energy markets. EU consumers spend €1 billion per month more than they should on energy because the market is not liberalised. Competition would bring benefits to consumers, and promote the competitiveness of EU energy companies in the world.

¿ How   meet

                          challenge   ?
                          _____

    Europe

                          must modernise

                          to be competitive

                          _____

    This is why

    PM s + Pres
                          OK d

                                       ambitious goals
                                       (LISBON)

                          _____

---

    aim

                    = _/

    make

                     Europe

                                 competitive
                                 by 2010

                          _____

¿ What   do

                     to achieve   ?
                     _____

Dates

Dates are often very important. They are used to compare "then" with "now", or "then" with another "then". Speakers use them to show progress over time, to make a point more dramatically. It is often useful to have them stand out on the page, and the margin is the best place for that. In the following example the speaker is clearly emphasising the year 1973 (so that he can compare it to the present day).

Example (**MacShane 1**)

And today? The changes, even since 1973, when Britain entered the European Economic Community, are remarkable:

The Europe of 1973 with its border control on goods and cars has gone. The myriad of currencies and currency controls acting as a blockage to fair, transparent, effective business has been replaced by a single market. One where the majority of EU citizens sensibly use one currency - the Euro.

The Europe of 1973 with dirty beaches, and expensive air travel and telephone calls has been replaced by a Europe which allows more people to travel, talk to each other and enjoy a shared and better-protected natural environment than ever before.

	changes		
	(since 1973)		
		are	
			remarkable
		_____	
1973	*Europe* *(border controls)*		
		has gone	
		_____	
	currencies + *curr controls*		
	(block *fair* *transp ^{t} bus ^{ns})* *effec ^{v}*		

Immediately the speaker's desire to compare 1973 with the present day becomes clear, and we stress it in our interpretation, because it is in the margin.

Anything important

There are no rules to note-taking, only ideas that can help, which you choose to use or not. Consequently, if you feel that something said is particularly important and needs to stand out very clearly in your notes, try putting it in the margin.

6.   Implicit Links

Links represent the relationship between one idea and another. Often they are flagged up by the speaker through their use of what are sometimes called "link words". But, as we saw in Chapter 4, this term can be misleading. The link is not a word; words can be used to highlight it, they are very useful pointers, but it is not the word that makes the link, it is the speaker's train of thought. Speakers may use no more than their intonation to flag up links. They may assume, because it is clear from the context, that the audience sees a link. Alternatively, they may use a word that we associate with a link where there is no link. It is also possible that the use and frequency of links in the target language differs slightly from that in the source language. It is up to you, the interpreter, to recognize and analyse these factors correctly. This is not the place to try and suggest how, that is for you and your teachers and colleagues to discuss. Below are just a few examples to point you in the right direction.

Adding links

Example (Torry 1)

> Britain and Germany are among those countries pushing most for an ambitious new WTO round. So, for both the UK and Germany, the failure of the trade talks in Cancun was a huge disappointment. A successful trade round would be a massive prize. If we could halve world tariffs, [then] that would add as much as $400 billion annually to world incomes, of which at least 150 billion will flow to developing countries. That's more than 3 times what they currently get in aid. But to achieve this we need to reform the CAP. There is a clear joint interest here between Britain and Germany.

Look at the last two sentences. There is no explicit link between *"But to achieve this we need to reform the CAP."* and *"There is a clear joint interest here between Britain and Germany."* But the speaker has spent the entire paragraph arriving at this conclusion (that, "[as a result of all that]" there is a "joint interest") so there is a link, and interpreters are well within their rights to note it as such. This clear notation will give you the choice, when you reproduce the speech, of rendering the link implicitly as well, through correct intonation, or rendering the link explicitly if you feel it is appropriate.

```
┌──────────┬──────────────────────────────────────────┐
│          │                                          │
│   B      │   need                                   │
│          │                                          │
│          │              reform                      │
│          │                                          │
│          │                          CAP             │
│          │                                          │
│          │              _____                 │
│          │                                          │
│   →      │                                          │
│          │   joint interest                         │
│          │                                          │
└──────────┴──────────────────────────────────────────┘
```

The same technique can be used to deal with "if" clauses in English.

Example (**Torry 1**)

> If we could halve world tariffs, that would add as much as $400 billion annually to world incomes, of which at least 150 billion will flow to developing countries.

In English the speaker is not required to follow an "if" clause with the word "then". But that does not mean that the causal relationship between the two halves of the sentence disappears. Below, the word "*then*" has been added to the text. Note, however, that both versions mean the same thing.

> If we could halve world tariffs, **[then]** that would add as much as $400 billion annually to world incomes, of which at least 150 billion will flow to developing countries.

In our notes the symbol for "consequence", and for *then* in this example is → . So the passage above is noted as below.

Interpreters can add to their notes the link which is implicit so that it is clearer to them. The link may remain implicit in your spoken version as well, but because it was explicit in the notes, you will follow the speaker's reasoning more easily when you read back your notes and also give the correct intonation to this part of the speech, so that your audience also recognize the link.

Dropping "link words" that aren't links

The words that usually represent links are often used by speakers in other ways. Don't blindly let the word trap you into noting a link where there is none, or into noting an incorrect link.

Example (**Torry 1**)

> In Britain we envy Germany's training system for example. Or the high productivity of its workers. We can learn from Germany's successes here.
> And in Britain we have had successes too.
> Getting the long term unemployed back into work has been a major success.

The word *And* in *And in Britain* is certainly not a link of addition. In fact it is more like a link of contradiction, a "but" if anything at all. If you note it as such the speaker's message will be clearer to you when you read back you notes.

	We
	can learn from
	DE successes
	_____
BUT	*UK also*
	has successes
	_____

The bottom line will always be understanding what the speaker is trying to say. Adding or deleting links incorrectly will mean you saying something different to the speaker.

7 Pro-forms[§]

What is a pro-form? For the purposes of our note-taking, following Andres (2000), we will take it to mean a lexical unit that refers back, not just to one person, or object, but to a whole passage, a whole idea, or series of events. We have seen that if you want to refer back to a single word or symbol, then you should use the recall line (see Part II, page 133). But look at the extract below.

Example (**Torry 1**)

> So how are we to meet this challenge?
> In a globalised world, Europe needs to modernise and reform if it is to remain competitive. **It was for this reason** that the Heads of State and Government of the European Union agreed in Lisbon in 2000 a series of ambitious goals.

The pro-form is marked in bold. What does the expression *it was for this reason* it refer back to? Why did the Heads of State and Government agree ambitious goals in Lisbon? Because, *in a globalised world, Europe needs to modernise and reform if it is to remain competitive.* The words *it was for this reason* refer to a whole idea, not only to one noun. Let's take another example.

Example (**Hodgson**)

> And the key thing to remember about climate change is that it is a cumulative process. If the rate and magnitude of climate change is not slowed down by a reduction in greenhouse gas emissions, any beneficial effects are expected to diminish while the costs and risks continue to increase. The negative effects predominate in the longer term.
> **This is why** New Zealand can't afford to ignore climate change – and why we can't refuse to play our part, however small, in trying to do something about it.

The words *this is why* refer here to a whole paragraph about the cumulative nature of climate change and the threats that poses.

So why are pro-forms important for us when noting in consecutive? These two examples are relatively straightforward, and the pro-forms are flagged up by the obliging use of the expressions, *it was for this reason* and *this is why*. It is very unlikely that you will miss them, either when listening or when reading back your notes, especially if you take the easy option and note *this why* in your notes. However, pro-forms are not always so obliging and the words *it* and *this* are just as likely to be used as the two expressions above. It these cases interpreters have to spot the reference and mark it in their notes, so that the same reference is clear to the audience when the interpreter speaks, which is after all the point of their work! This makes it more difficult. Note simply *it* or *this* in your notes and you could be in real trouble when you come to read them back, as it may no longer be clear what they refer to.

There is a very simple strategy for dealing with pro-forms, which in no way disturbs the structure of our notes. On the right-hand side of the page, where it won't interfere with the rest of your notes, draw a large close bracket **/** on the right of the page, alongside the idea(s) to which reference is made. The height of the bracket should be such that the ideas referred to fall between its top and bottom. To the right of that, draw a line from the centre of the bracket, to the place later in your notes where reference is made. See the example below, taken from the first text above.

Example (Torry 1)

So how are we to meet this challenge?
In a globalised world, Europe needs to modernise and reform if it is to remain competitive.
It was for this reason that the Heads of State and Government of the European Union agreed in Lisbon in 2000 a series of ambitious goals.

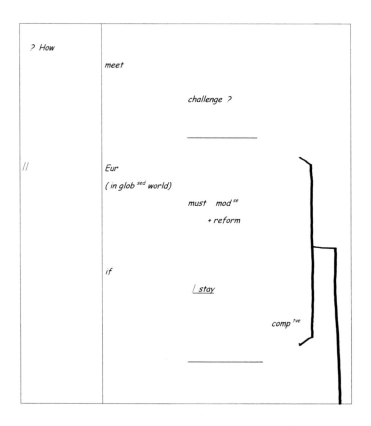

Figure 6

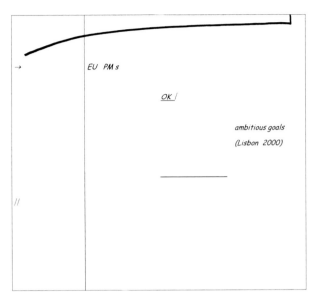

Figure 7

The line can be taken to the next page without risking confusion, as in the example. In fact, by their very nature, pro-forms will often occur quite some time later in the speech and the interpreter will be obliged to make the link between two things on different pages of notes.

Example (**MacShane 2**)

We want to Europeanise the Balkans, not Balkanise Europe.
Romania, Britain and the other 26 independent, sovereign nations that form the Intergovernmental Conference are working on the answer. Prime Ministers Nastase* and Blair and other Heads of Government were in Rome earlier this week to start the process off. And Messrs Geoana and Straw* and their Foreign Minister counterparts will continue it.

* Mr Nastase is Prime Minister of Romania, Mr Geona is the Romanian Foreign Minister. Jack Straw is the UK Foreign Minister.

Now we could note this passage as follows:

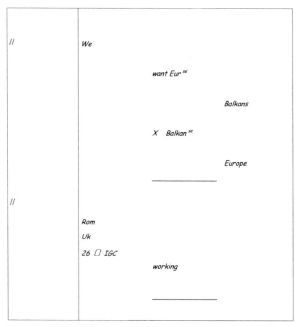

Figure 8

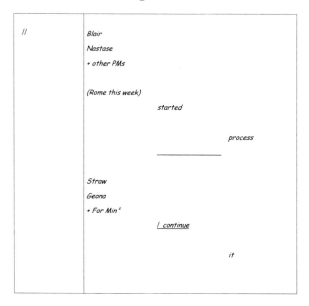

Figure 9

But look at this *it*! What does *it* refer to? The interpreter might just like to say it, but most of the time it is helpful to know what something refers to. Here *it* refers to process, but of course this doesn't help us. What does process refer to? It refers back to *Europeanizing the Balkans* which is some time earlier in the speech.

To make things clear, quickly, to the interpreter so that they can make it clear to their audience we can do as follows,

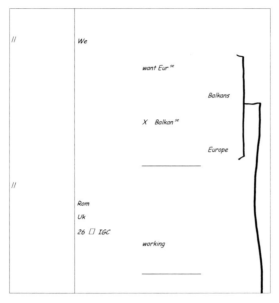

Figure 10

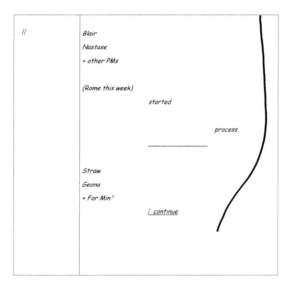

Figure 11

If you are using the page-turning technique described on page 73, you will see that the two parts of the line join up across the two pages.

8.   Noting sooner, or later

You are not obliged to note what you hear in the same order as you hear it, and if you stick to the structures and layout explained in Part I you will have some room for manoeuvre. You can allow yourself to remember what is easy to remember, noting it later or not at all, and write down quickly what is more difficult to remember without getting your notes in a muddle.

Noting detail sooner

Things which are difficult to remember and might be noted down as soon as you hear them, (and not in the same order you heard them) are outlined in Chapter 8: what to note and include, names, dates, numbers and technical terminology (page 120). Whether a given detail is important or not in the context of a speech is something you have to work out for yourself.

Example (**Hodgson**)

> For those of you who don't know me, I'm the Minister of Energy, Science, Fisheries and a few other things including climate change policy. It's that last one that has taken me up close and personal with dairy farmers and brought me the invitation to speak here today.

When you hear this, you would be well advised to skip the words *For those of you who don't know me, I'm the…* and start noting the list of areas for which he is responsible minister, as this is likely to be more important. It will be easy to remember that he is a Minister, so we start by noting his areas of competence, then later we add *Minister*. Start that list of areas of competence towards the right of the page so that you can add rest on the left, in the SVO set up, later. So your notes will look like this,

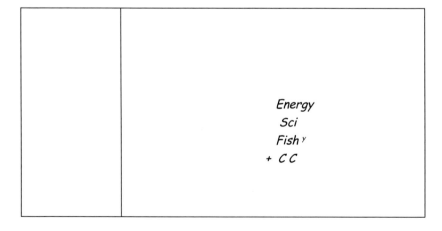

and then you continue. Below I have marked the chronological order in which these elements are noted in square brackets [ ].

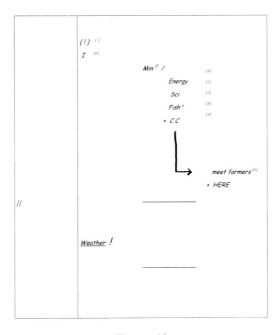

Figure 12

Word order

The same applies in inflected languages like German and Polish where stylistic inversions of the normal Subject Verb Object word order are common. In this case you should note these elements in the order you hear them, BUT change their position on the page so that you still have SVO from left to right on your pad. Otherwise you risk making a mistake in your rendition of the speech.

The speaker's word order may be *Object Verb Subject* but our notes still look like this. You will have noted the elements in the order you heard them (given in square brackets [1]), but positioned them on the page as below.

Subject [3]	
	Verb [2]
	Object [1]
	_____

***Example* (Buzek)**

> To właśnie od tempa prac dostosowawczych będzie zależał w dużej mierze postęp negocjacji, a, co za tym idzie, także data przystąpienia Polski do Unii Europejskiej.

Literally in English this reads,

> On the speed of harmonisation will depend to a great extent the progress in the negotiations and therefore also Poland's date of accession to the European Union.

But you will not note in the same order as you hear the words, you will recreate the SVO structure. This will give you the following notes. The order the notes would have been taken in is the same as the order on the page if you read from top to bottom and read left to right.

	progress in neg
+ so	*PL accession date*
	<u>*depend on*</u>
	speed / harm tn
	————

Noting detail later

Whereas above there was detail we held to be crucial and therefore noted immediately, there will also be times where the detail is less important, and, having noted the core ideas, you may decide to add an element of detail to your notes a little later on, if time allows. Having decided it is detail, and not central to the SVO group, where exactly you put the additional detail on the page is a matter of personal taste, as long as it doesn't disrupt the structure of the rest of the notes on the page. Again the order the elements were noted in this example is given in square brackets like this [1].

Example (**Patten**)

In the areas for which I have some responsibility, there were also, as the Prime Minister has mentioned, some important developments at Feira. We took stock of the European Union's relations with Russia and the situation there, including in Chechnya, in the light of the recent EU-Russia Summit, which I think was regarded as fairly successful.

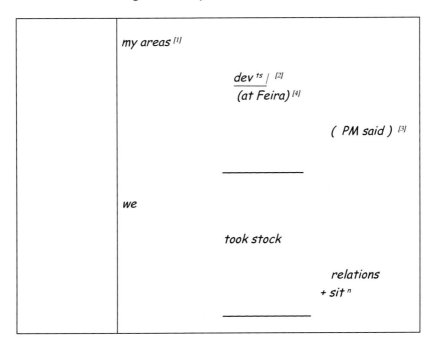

In this example you don't want to get caught up noting *"the PM said"* only to miss the more important part of the sentence, *"were also important developments"*, so when you have heard and analysed the whole section you can go back and add this to your notes, if you have time.

Noting lists

You will hear a list in order: 1, 2, 3. You will find, however, that it is possible to relieve the strain on your short-term memory by noting 1, 3, 2. This is because if you note 1 and 3 the moment you hear them, they never make it into your memory and therefore never burden it. All you have to do is remember 2 for a couple of seconds. This works with longer lists as well of course, but the exact order is something you will have to practise and work out for yourself. At the same time the elements of the list remain vertically aligned to one another as described in Chapter 5.

Example (**Hodgson**)

> For those of you who don't know me, I'm the Minister of Energy, Science, Fisheries and a few other things including climate change policy. It's that last one that has taken me up close and personal with dairy farmers and brought me the invitation to speak here today.

The example above could have been noted in the order below. I have marked the chronological order in which these elements are noted in square brackets like this [1]. The change in the order of noting elements in the list ([1] - [4]) as compared to the order in which they where spoken is minor but is very effective in relieving excess strain on your memory.

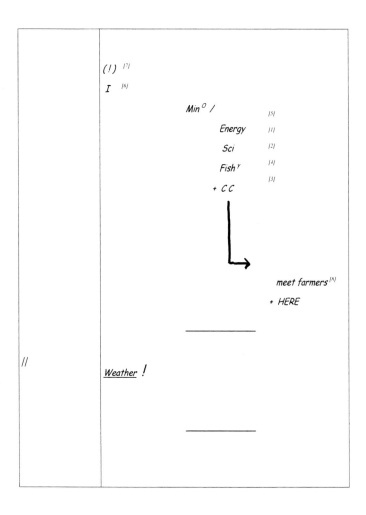

Figure 13

9.   How You Write it

Writing big and bigger

The size of what you note on the pad is not governed by any rules and you should use this freedom to give your notes extra clarity. If something is important then write it in bigger letters on the page. If you remember Chapter 4, you will see that this is what we did for links. In the example below, not only the links are noted in larger writing, but also the contrast between what *does* and *does not make sense*. This is what the speaker wants to get across and we can do that more easily if it is clear to us on the notepad page.

Example (**Torry 1**)

Different countries have different systems and structures, so a solution which works in one place will not necessarily work in another.
It doesn't make sense to regulate everything from Brussels.
But it does make sense to share our experience and to learn from each other.

→	*solution*
	may work
	in A
	not B
	———————
//	*regulate all*
	NOT make sense
	———————
B	*sharing experience + learning*
	DOES make sense
	———————

Capital letters for proper names

If a proper name also has meaning as a word in its own right, then when it is used as a name, note it in capital letters to avoid confusion. It will usually be very clear from the context which one is correct, but it is better to have a foolproof system in place before you find out the hard way that it isn't always clear. In the example below, a project is called "Reflex".

***Example* (MacShane 2)**

> But you can count on the UK and other EU partners to help you with them, provided the political commitment and direction is there. I'd like to give you an example. Yesterday I attended a reception linked to a successful UK/Romanian project called Project Reflex.

Phonetic spelling and misspelling

Another perfectly valid way of making life easier for yourself, by writing less, is to spell words phonetically rather than correctly or simply to misspell them. This is a technique that some interpreters use regularly, and which others don't like and don't use at all. The decision as to whether you use it is up to you.

This technique will also be of less use to those of you who note in a language that is written more or less phonetically anyway, like German or Polish, but will be more attractive to, say, French and English speakers where a phonetic transcription will often be shorter than the correct spelling.

Examples

light	lite
countries	country ˢ
children	child ˢ
before	b4

10. More on Symbols

Improvising symbols

In Chapter 6 we said that you shouldn't improvise symbols while you are working as you are most likely to forget what the new symbol actually represents and therefore make a serious mistake. However, sometimes you may find yourself in a situation where the speaker is repeatedly talking about a concept which it is very long and slow to write down in words and for which you can think of a quick symbol. If this happens, the safest bet is to note some unmistakeable version of the offending concept (like the words in full) next to the new symbol but off to the right hand side of the page. There it will not interfere with the structure of your notes and when you come later to read back your notes you will have a reminder. In the example below we realize the term *climate change* is going to crop up again and again, so we note CC as our new symbol and the full version on the right. Every subsequent time it is mentioned we note only CC.

Example (**Hodgson**)

> But what I will tell you – and what a climatologist would tell you – is that this is what climate change looks like. One of the significant consequences expected from climate change is an increase in the frequency and severity of extreme weather events.

<table>
<tr><td>B</td><td>I

              will say</td></tr>
</table>

B	I	*will say*
	∩ *c c*	*climate change*
		= *similar*
		—————————
//	*1 result*	
		=
		more storms
		—————————
→	...	

Symbol of relation /

Discussions are *about* something; reports, comments and policies are *on* something; attitudes and reactions *to* something; responsibility, permits, contracts and authorisation *for* something;

     All the prepositions in italics can be noted clearly and simply with the same symbol / .

a report on the economy	a discussion about future of Europe	a contract for reconstruction work

rpt
  / *economy*
	"
	        /
	       Eur
		contract
		       /
		    reconst^{tn}

Not only, but also …

This little expression crops up with quite improbable frequency on the floors of meeting rooms around the globe. The following is a very simple, but visually striking way of noting it, so that when you read back your notes you will be able to give the audience the same impression as the speaker gave in his original. The trick to getting your intonation right is reading ahead, as described in the section Moving On… and seeing the *but also* as you read your notes for the *not only*. This example shows how that can be done.

***Example* (Torry 1)**

> We also need CAP reform - not just because it helps in the WTO - but, perhaps more important because the CAP is simply an inefficient, hugely expensive and unfair system.

		We	
			need
			CAP reform
		_____	
n.o.	*cos*	*reform*	
			helps
			WTO
b a	*cos*	*CAP*	
		=	
			inefficient
			expensive
			unfair

The exclamation mark

We have seen that the question mark may be placed in the margin to announce the arrival of a question. Its cousin, the exclamation mark, can be equally useful in note-taking to highlight the humorous or unusual nature of a remark.

In the first example, a speech given by a government Minister about the dangers of climate change, the suggestion that global warming might be a good thing is clearly at odds with the general view and perhaps also intended to raise a laugh from his audience. It can be noted as below.

Example **(Hodgson)**

> More than one farmer has suggested to me that a little global warming might not be such a bad thing for farming.

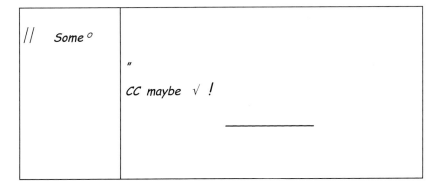

The exclamation mark can also be used as a memory prompt in line with what we saw in Chapter 7. It reminds us that something has not been noted and should be recalled from memory. In the following example the exclamation mark is enough to help us recall the compliment made by the speaker to his Bulgarian hosts and then the details surrounding the *footnote*. The exclamation mark is also an indicator to the interpreter that a more elaborate style of language is to be used when rendering this section of the speech.

Example **(MacShane 1)**

> So on the sands of the Black Sea, the contacts were re-established, and over a glass of the wonderful wine that Bulgaria has the genius to produce, my footnote in the history of Europe's liberation from communism continued to be written.

→

recontact

(wine *!*)

footnote *!*
----------→

+
_____

11.   Things You Didn't Catch

Yes, it will happen. You will be concentrating on one thing and another will pass you by. This will happen more often while you're learning than later. But it won't stop happening the day you pass your final exams. So how do you deal with the situation?

Omissions

If, for lack of time, you can't manage to note something you would like to, make sure you mark the place very clearly so that at least your memory has a chance to reconstruct the missing information. This is particularly easy with lists. Let's imagine that in the example below you had missed one of the adjectives towards the end, for example, *hugely expensive*. If you note the omission as a hyphen in the list, as in the example below, you will at least know when you read back your notes that something is missing, and from context and with the help of your memory you have a good chance of recalling what.

Example (**Torry 1**)

> We also need CAP reform - not just because it helps in the WTO - but, perhaps more important because the CAP is simply an inefficient, hugely expensive and unfair system.

		We			
			need		
					CAP reform
			────────		
n.o.	*cos*	*reform*			
			helps		
					WTO
b a	*cos*	*CAP*			
			=		
					inefficient
					-
					unfair
			────────		

Questions to the speaker

This is a subject on which there are as many opinions as there are interpreters! Sometimes you will find that you have failed to note or hear properly something that was clearly important to the speech. Whether you ask a question of the speaker or not will depend a lot on the situation you are working in. If it is a small working group touring a building and getting on well with one another, you may decide that a question to the speaker is appropriate in order to get things right. It may even help your rapport with your clients. If, however, one dignitary is speaking at some ceremonial event in front of a captive audience of dozens or more people, it is unlikely that the situation is going to be conducive to your interrupting proceedings to ask a question. As far as accreditation tests for large institutions are concerned, one or even two questions are sometimes allowed, but candidates must be careful, having asked the question, then to get that bit of the speech right! Deciding whether to ask a question will always be a tough call that you will have to make on the spot.

Before you make that decision though, make sure that you can find the part of your notes you may be about to ask a question on. Here are two techniques that work:

- mark a big **X** on the right hand side of the page AND then leave your spare pen or pencil between the pages in question as a bookmark.

- mark a big **X** on the right hand side of the page AND fold the offending page of your notepad diagonally across itself so that it sticks out of the side of the rest of the pad and can be found again immediately when you are looking for it later.

If you decide to ask a question, make sure it is in the speaker's language, clear and succinct. You should ask politely for specifics, e.g. "Could you please repeat the date on which the company opened offices in Cologne?" and not for general explanation. A question like, "I didn't understand the bit about the new marketing strategy" is unacceptable anywhere.

Techniques like this should be practised in the safety of the classroom before being used at work or in examinations. They must be incorporated into your general presentation technique, and never give the impression of incompetence or disarray.

12   The End

The last thing the speaker says

I am sure you are relieved to reach the end of this book, and you will be relieved whenever a speaker gets to the end of what they have to say. But be careful not to let your guard down too soon. The chances are that the very last thing the speaker says will be quite important. It may be a punchy slogan; it may be the essence of everything that has gone before it in the speech; it may be an appeal to the audience based on what has just been said. It may be all of these things or something else, but most speakers like to go out with a bang and so it is very likely that it will be an important part of the speech. You can usually hear the end coming in a speech. When you do, listen to it even more carefully than you have been listening already. You may even want to stop taking notes and only listen for a moment. Once they have grasped what has been said, many interpreters will write out this part of the speech in much more detail, even in a virtually longhand translation, just to make sure they will get it right in their version. Remember, the speaker will have stopped speaking by now, so you will have a few seconds of extra time to do this, (although you don't want to keep the audience waiting while you scribble away for minutes).

The end of your notes

There is nothing worse than turning over a page in your notes and being surprised to find nothing there. When you are working from your notes you will want some warning that the end is approaching.
When you listen to a speaker speak, you can hear when they start to wind up as they approach the end of their speech. The speech will not just stop, but will build towards a conclusion for which the audience have been well prepared by the speaker. The same audience will need to hear the same progression towards an ending in the interpreter's version. To help, you will need to include a clear signal that the end is approaching in your notes. The simplest way is to draw not one (as we usually do) but two or three horizontal lines across the page. If you are using the page-turning technique described on page 73, this will give you a page or so of warning that the end is in sight and you can start working up towards it yourself.

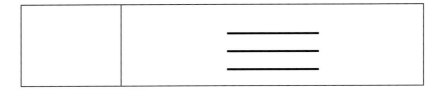

PART III

The Back of the Book

1.   Notes with Commentary

Here you will find a series of example notes taken from extended extracts of speeches which you have already come across in Parts I and II. These notes show how each speech might have been noted if the techniques described in Parts I and II are applied. They are not, however, to be considered as the only correct way to apply those techniques nor as the only way to note these source speeches. They are examples and no more.

After each page of notes I offer comments describing the technique used for a selected piece of notation. Each technique is commented on only on its first appearance in the notes below and not later. For the first speech I have suggested a literal reading of the notes.

Where applicable, information on the Internet sites where you can find the full texts of the speeches used here is given on pages 226 "Examples".

Speech 1   Hodgson

1.

For those of you who don't know me, I'm the Minister of Energy, Science, Fisheries and a few other things including climate change policy. It's that last one that has taken me up close and personal with dairy farmers and brought me the invitation to speak here today. So let's talk about the weather.

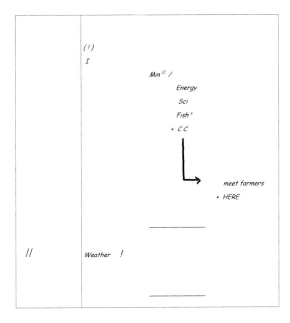

Figure 14

Literally the notes read,
I, Minister for Energy, Science, Fisheries, Climate Change which brings me to meet farmers and to here
Weather

a) *(!)* — The comment *for those of you who don't know me* is not really worth noting, or indeed reproducing in interpretation, as it is a meaningless filler. But, if you like, you could signal the presence of a remark like this with the exclamation mark in brackets.

b) — The verb *to be* need not be noted when the subject of the verb is obvious, here *I am*.

c) *Min* ^{o} — The raised ^{o} denotes *person*.

d) *C C* — Knowing in advance the topic of the conference we decide that *climate change* is going to be mentioned frequently but that it is too long to note in full each time. This might be your symbol, or abbreviation, for the day (Chapter 6). He is a Minister talking about his responsibilities, so *policy* should be clear from context and we don't note it.

e) *Energy*
Sci
Fish ^{y}
+ C C
— The speaker is Minister of all these things equally, they are of equal value, so they are noted parallel to one another on the page (Chapter 5).

f) → — Note that this is not a recall line, because it has an arrow attached to the end of it. The arrow signifies cause and effect, and indeed, *It is CC that brings me here*.

g) // — There is a clear break here, and we mark it as such in the notes. This non-link is noted larger than the rest of the notes also, so that it stands out even more.

h) *Weather !* — The exclamation mark reminds us of intonation and saves us writing any notes. It is proportionally larger than the rest of the notes to attract our attention.

i) ——— — Even though the second section of notes is made up of only one word, it still follows and begins with a horizontal line across the page. In this way it will not be mistakenly amalgamated into the ideas immediately preceding or following it.

2.

> I'm not about to tell you that the storms we're going through now are the result of climate change. I'm not a climatologist and I don't think even a climatologist would offer any conclusions on that score.

//	X ⌐" ∩ *storms now* <div align="right">cos C C</div> <div align="right">———————</div>
// (	*Even Clim* ° (I m X ...) <div align="right">^ X ⌐"</div>
)	<div align="center">———————</div>

Literally the notes read:

> *will not say that*
> *storms now [are] because of climate change*
> *Even climatologist (and I am not one) would not say*

a) ( )   This section is a digression from the main part of the speech, (*I won't say ...but what I will say is...*). The brackets that signal this were added after the section had been noted and when it had become clear that this was an aside.

b) X ⌐"   I will not say = *I'm not about to tell you.*

c) *Clim* °   A person from the noun *Climate* = climatologist.

d)   ∩   = *that*, introducing a clause (Part II Clauses).

e)   (*I m*   The fact of his not being a climatologist is secondary so after
      X ...)   hearing and noting the rest of the idea we add it in the brackets and
                     below *Clim ⁰* to make this clear and help us arrive at the correct
                     intonation in the production phase.

f)   X ⌐ ″   *wouldn't say* (Part II Verbs).

g)   In these first two pages of notes, and those that follow, note how much
                     space is left on the notepad page, how the notes are not cramped and
                     how the structure is clearly visible as you read.

3.
      But what I will tell you – and what a climatologist would
tell you – is that this is what climate change looks like. One of
the significant consequences expected from climate change is an
increase in the frequency and severity of extreme weather events.
This is why we use the term climate change in preference to global warming,

Literally the notes read,

> *But I will say*
> *that climate change is similar*
> *One result is more storms*
> *therefore we say climate change not global warming*

a) **B**   You can see that the links stand out very clearly when noted in larger writing at the left of the page. This makes reading them back easier. **B** = *but* = all links of contradiction with a following limitation. (See Chapter 4). Here the contradiction is with the idea expressed two sections earlier in the notes, *I won't say ...but what I will say is...*

b) *climatologist*   Given what has gone before we can rely on memory to give us the repeated mention of *climatologist*. Don't worry about forgetting things, but you could also note an empty pair of brackets below *I* to remind you. **( )**

c) **S V O**   The second two sections of notes show very clearly the diagonal Subject Object Verb structure on the page.

d) *will say*   Here the *will* is not a future tense but an expression of the speaker's opinion, so it is noted it in full to avoid confusion.

e) *more storms*   We do not need to write *the frequency and severity of extreme weather events* in our notes. Note the simple for the complicated. Two words to sum it up will suffice. That does not mean that we will only say „storms" when we give back the speech but that it will be enough to remind us of the broader and wordier expression.

f) →   Here the words were *This is why*. The underlying meaning is, *leads to, has as a consequence*, etc.

g) **" C C "**   The inverted commas show that these are terms, here the speaker is talking about the terminology, not the concepts.

h) *warm ᵍ*   The *g* is raised as an abbreviation of *–ing*

4.

because it more accurately captures the range of climatic effects that the enhanced greenhouse effect is expected to produce. A long-term increase in global average temperatures is the key indicator and consequence of the build-up of greenhouse gases in the Earth's atmosphere. But the expected effects of that change on the world's climate systems are multiple and diverse.

cos	*this term*	
	$=$	
		more accur
		————
//	*↗ temp*	
	$=$	
		indic
		+ effect
		(↑ gas)
		————
B	*effects*	
	$=$	
		mult
		+ divr ˢ
		————

Literally the notes read,

> *because this term is more accurate*
> *rise in temperature is indicator and effect of increase in gas*
> *but effects are multiple and diverse*

a)   *long term*   The words *long term* are not noted here. Our general knowledge will supply them during the production phase.

b)   *indic*   *indicator* underlined gives us *key indicator*.

 (↑ gas)   This is easily sufficient to jog our memory (from some basic general knowledge) as to what type of gases and where they are accumulating.

5.

The New Zealand dairy industry is founded on the superb conditions this country's climate provides for growing grass. This is why climate change matters to dairy farmers and – because of the economic importance of your industry – to New Zealand.

// →	NZ dairy ind
	
	based on
	
	                     great clim
	           ————
	
	C C
	           ==
	                     to farmers
	                     + to NZ

Literally the notes read,

New Zealand Dairy industry is based on great climate
so climate change is important to farmers and to New Zealand

a)   ==   = *important.*

6.

We know climate change is already under way on a global scale and there do appear to be some measurable effects emerging in New Zealand. A study done for the Ministry for the Environment said a southward shift in subtropical pasture species might be one indicator, along with an increased frequency of warmer winters in recent decades

Ō

C C

<u>start</u>/

AND

effects

in NZ

_____

// Study
(Min Env)

"

∩

↓ S

/ sub trop   past ʳ species

+   ↑ warm winters

=

indicator

_____

Literally the notes read,

Know that climate change has started
and there are effects in New Zealand
A Ministry of Environment study says that
the move Southwards of subtropical pasture species and the warmer
winters are an indicator {of this}

a)   Ō

to know. ∩ is not noted for (*to know) that*, as it is obvious here. Later on this page we do note ∩ as that section of the notes is more complex and we want the notes to be clear.

b)   ∩

We can split the idea from its clause across two pages so that we don't risk cramping our notes in at the bottom of the page. This symbol signals that what follows is part of the same idea. If you use the techniques for turning the pages of your pad on page 73, you can continue fluently from one page to the next.

c)   (Min Env)

The information about who commissioned the study is interesting, and important, but fundamentally secondary so it goes into brackets.

d)   ∕

This very useful symbol can get you out of many a tight spot. Here it showing what *moved southwards* -

e)   ↓ S
         ↑ warm winters

These two elements are parallel with one another on the page as they are both equal consequences (*indicators*) of global warming.

7.

It also suggested that a recorded halving of the planted area in kiwifruit in Northland over the six years to 2001 could be at least partly attributable to a warming climate, leading to reduced productivity. More than one farmer has suggested to me that a little global warming might not be such a bad thing for farming. And it is true that warmer average temperatures could bring some benefits, including better pasture growth in milder winters.

ALSO ∩

$\frac{1}{2}$ area kiwi
  Northland
  6 → 2001

= cos C C
(→ ↓ prod ^{ty})
_____

|| Some ^{o}

"

CC maybe √ !

_____

(true
↑ temp   →   benefits
                   (pastures)

) _____

Literally the notes read,

> *also [says] that the halving of area of kiwi fruit in the 6 years up to 2001*
> *is the result of climate change,(which has caused lower productivity)*
> *Some people may say that climate change is a good thing*
> *True temperatures rise which leads to benefits, e.g. for pastures*

a) (}
)

This digression should not be dwelled on by the interpreter, the brackets show that the whole section is an aside to be spoken with less emphasis.

b) *CC maybe* √ !   ! denotes irony.

c) *Northland*   Unfamiliar proper names should be noted in full if you have time.

8.

Some of the predicted impacts of a moderate rate of climate change for Taranaki include changes in average temperature and rainfall patterns, and a rise in sea levels. In general, Taranaki, like much of the west coast of New Zealand, is likely to become warmer and wetter – perhaps up to 3°C warmer, on average, over the next 70-100 years.

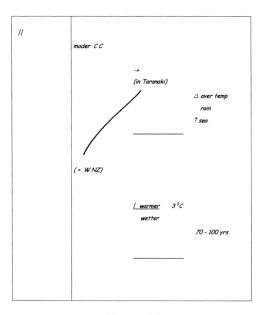

Figure 15

Literally the notes read,

> *Moderate climate change lead to (in Taranaki) change in average temperature, rainfall and sea level.*
> *Taranaki and Western New Zealand will get warmer by 3C and wetter in next 70-100 years*

a)   △   = change.

b)   △ *aver temp*   List of elements of equal value, so they are parallel on the
       rain   page. The words *patterns* and *level* don't need to be noted as
       ↑ *sea*   these are the obvious collocations with *rain and temperature*
                          and *sea* in this context.

c)   *3° C*   Was noted after the *70 - 100 yrs*. Added later, if you like,
                          as a detail once the main Subject Verb Object group had been
                          understood and committed to paper.

Speech 2   Patten

1.

>In the areas for which I have some responsibility, there were also, as the Prime Minister has mentioned, some important developments at Feira. We took stock of the European Union's relations with Russia and the situation there, including in Chechnya, in the light of the recent EU-Russia Summit, which I think was regarded as fairly successful.

	my areas
	$\underline{\underline{}}$ *dev^s*
	(at Feira)　　*(PM __"|__)*
	_____
look |	
	EU-RU relat ^{n}s
	+ sit ^{n}
	(Chec)
	(EU RU summit
	__√__)
	_____

a)	$\underline{\underline{}}$	Double underlining = important.
b)	*(at Feira)* *(PM __"|__)*	These two elements are not part of the S V O group and can be noted wherever we are comfortable having them on the page.
c)		Don't need to note the Subject *we* as it is obvious from context.

d)   *look |*   Simpler and shorter for *took stock.*

e)   (*Chec*)   This is additional information, as shown by the word
                                           including, so it is in brackets in the notes, and we can fit
          (*EU RU summit*   it back into our version as appropriate when reading back
                ⎽√⎽   )   our notes.

f)   ⎽√⎽   A tick for positive, underlined with a broken line to
                                           denote *fairly.*

2.

        It is too early to judge President Putin's economic programme; however,
        our basic message is that a sound programme will be vital to boost investor
        confidence.

//	
	too early
	to judge
	econ prog
	_____
B	*message* =
	∩
	sound prog
	| imp[t]
	↗ *inv* ° *confid*
	_____

a)   //   No link.

b) $\underline{\underline{/ \, imp^t}}$

The symbol for a future tense, plus the adjective, underlined twice gives us, *will be very important,* = *vital.* We note the underlying meaning of *vital* (*very important*) rather than the word itself. This will give us more choice when choosing a word in our production phase. To avoid confusion with the symbol denoting the future tense $\underline{/}$ we may decide here not to use a double underlining alone $\underline{\underline{}}$ for *important* (as in Speech 1.5 above) but a conventional abbreviation instead.

c) $\cap$

Introduction of a clause. *Our message is THAT* ($\cap$).

3.

On Chechnya, there have, it is true, been some recent moderately positive developments in response to international and European Union pressure: for example the recent ECHO mission was able to take place and western humanitarian agencies have greater access to the area. The conflict nevertheless continues and we still have considerable concerns.

// Chec	
	$\sqrt{}$ $\underline{dev^s \; /}$
	cos pressure -
	-
eg	ECHO mission
	agencies ↗ access
	_____
B	conflict
	- - - - - - - - - →
+	concerned
	_____

a)   *Chec*   In the margin because it is important in this speech.

b)   _√_   *moderately* is expressed in the notes by the broken
     - - - - - -   underlining.

c)   *pressure* -   The dashes show me there are two elements here, we are
              -         banking on memory to reproduce *EU* and *International*,
                        which shouldn't be too difficult in this context.

d)   *pressure*   We might have noted **press** here as an abbreviation of
                        pressure, but that could lead to confusion with *media*, so the
                        whole word is noted.

e)   *agencies*   From context you will be able recall that these are humanitarian
                        agencies (and that the speaker is, therefore, probably talking
                        about Western ones).

f)   *concerned*   This word, an adjective, is the same as the past participle of
                        the verb *concern* but noted differently (not _*concern* |_)
                        to avoid a possible confusion of the two.

4.

In particular, we want to see much greater access for humanitarian aid
agencies. We want to see genuinely independent investigation into reports of
human rights abuses, and we want to see a real dialogue between the Russian
government and the Chechens.

eg	♥
	↗ *access*
	agencies
	indep investig[n]
	/
	HR abuse
	dial[g] *RU-Chec*
	_____

a)	♥	*want*
b)	*eg*	*in particular* means the same as *an important example* so we can note *eg* and underline it.
c)	↗ *access* *indep* *dial ⁹*	3 elements are parallel on the page as they are a list of things the EU wants to see happen.
d)	/	About, on, into
e)	*Chec*	Although from this context it should be clear do not note *Ch* for *Chechnya* because that might be your abbreviation for *China.*

Speech 3   Torry 1

1.

The success of the economic reform programme in Germany is of critical importance not just to Germany, but to the whole of Europe, and obviously to the UK.

Not surprisingly, when I talk to people in London, the major question on everybody's minds about Germany was: how serious is the state of the German economy?

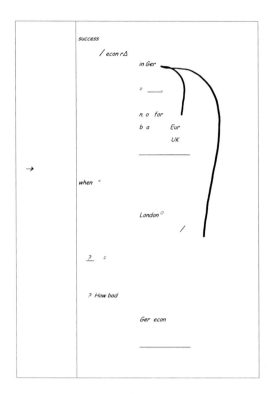

Figure 16

a) **/**   *of,* as in *success of the reform* AND then later *about,* as in,
                                    talk about Germany.

b) **rΔ**   *Δ* = change, *rΔ* = reform. See Chapter 6, Organic Symbols.

                                    The underlying meaning of the words *not surprisingly* is *so,*
c) **→**   *that's why,* and we don't want to get tangled up noting a long
                                    word like *surprisingly* for no good reason.

                                    We draw two recall lines from the abbreviation for Germany
                                    for two subsequent mentions, but at the bottom of the page
d) **Double recall**   we note *Ger* again because a third line might make the notes
    line   less clear. Don't use the recall line for its own sake, only to
                                    make your notes quicker and clearer.

                                    not only... but also. Always note the full stop after *n.* and *o.*
                                    to avoid confusion with *no.* There is similar risk with *b a* so
e) **n. o.**   to save time we don't note the full stops. The two are noted
    b a   parallel on the page as the two elements they precede will be
                                    of equal value.

f)   *London* °   People in London.

g)   <u>?</u>   =   *the major question on everybody's minds about Germany was* See how this can be boiled down in our notes, literally the notes read, *big question is,* with the underlining denoting *big.*

2.

     People don't just ask this question in the UK because of the commercial importance of the German market. The German economy, the biggest in the euro area, is also of great symbolic significance.

     You all know ...

//	*ask*
	n. o. *cos* *Ger* =
	trade imp^t
	(biggest in Euro)
	b a *cos*
	symbolic
	_____
//	*Ō*

a)   *Ger*   We need not note *economy* as it is clear from context that this is what the speaker is talking about.

b)   *n.o.*   *b a*   The *not only, but also* is less obvious here, but it is still there! Spotting this sort of thing is what taking notes in consecutive is all about.

c)   *Euro*   This is not the same as the symbol for Europe, *(Eur)* or for the EU *(EU)* so it is clear that this is the Eurozone.

d)   *cos*
     symbolic   The repetition of *Germany* in your notes is unnecessary. At a push you could use a recall line but even that is not really needed - it is clear we're still talking about Germany.

e)   *Ō*   = *You know.* The notes run onto the next page here, but because there is no horizontal line across the page we know that there is no break in speech.

f)   *end of the page*   The end of the page is not the end of an idea, there is no line across the page and you don't want to pause when giving your rendition either.

3.

   that the British Government would like to join the euro once the five economic tests are met.

   But selling the decision to the British public in a referendum will be difficult, if the eurozone economies, with Germany at the head, are seen to be performing badly.

```
          ∩
          UK

                    wants join

                              EURO

                              ( 5 tests )

                    _____

 B        ref dum

                         | diff

 if       EURO econs
          ( Ger )

                    X perform


                    _____
```

a)　(5 tests)　　A very limited grasp of European current affairs will be enough to know that the UK has said it wishes for 5 conditions to be met before it considers joining the Euro. If you didn't know that, get reading more newspapers!

b)　*B* ref dum *if*　　Together in one section of notes, (not split by a horizontal line), as they constitute two parts of one cause and effect relationship, *if x then y.*

c)　ref dum diff　　Language like *selling the decision* need not be noted. In fact the notes here read *referendum will be difficult* and this should be enough to remind us of the rest.

4.

　　If on the other hand they are undertaking structural reforms which are dealing with the problems they face, promoting the euro in the UK is a much easier task.

　　Ladies and Gentlemen,

　　Let me say something about the other common interests I mentioned.

//	
B	
if	struct ^{al} rΔ (→ tackle)
→	easy
	_____
//	♥ "
	/
	other common int
	_____

a) **Easy** | Detail like *in the UK* and *the Euro* are obvious from context and don't need to be noted. This is essentially just the opposite of the previous paragraph about *difficult to sell* - see Chapter 7, Memory prompts.

b) **//** | *Ladies and Gentleman* need not to be noted, this is a device the speaker is using to indicate to listeners that he has moved onto a new part of the speech, so we note it like this. Whether the interpreter actually says *Ladies and Gentleman,* or merely pauses to mark the break, is irrelevant, as long as the audience are clear that a new section of the speech has begun.

c) **♥ "** | = *want to talk.* Again the notes take up the underlying meaning of the original ignoring the exact words used (*let me say something*).

5.

I mentioned EU enlargement; budgetary and CAP reform; action to deal with illegal immigration and bogus asylum seekers; trade liberalization; and security and defence.

One thing is remarkable about all of these common interests: we approach them together, through the European Union.

//

     "]

        /

        - *EU*↗

        - *r*Δ   */budget*
              /CAP

        - *action*
         / *illeg immig*
             bogus

        - *trade lib*

        - *sec* ^{ty} + *def*

//

1 thing !

all thru   EU

a)	*EU*↗	Enlargement.
b)	-	The first section is a list of 5, of which 2 items are split into 2 subsets. Note how the structure on the page reflects that. The hyphens were added later, when it became clear this was a longer list, to make it clearer which elements are parallel to which others.
c)	- *r*Δ */budget* */CAP*	Budget reform and CAP reform are two things, and together they have the "value" of one part of the list, so they are noted in a sub-list, one above vertically the other. Notice that the order in which the notes were taken is not the same as the order of the source speech. Compare with *security and defence* below.
d)	*sec* ^{ty} + *def*	Here *security and defence* is one thing, which happens to have two words in its title, and consequently is noted horizontally across the page.

e)   *bogus*   In context this word, which is often used in this context by English speakers, is enough to remind us of the rest.

6.

Fifty years ago, say, we would have tried to solve most of our problems with national policies.

There is much Germany and Britain can do together to address the shared challenges we face.

So let me turn to the first of the challenges I mentioned: EU enlargement.

// __50 yrs__ |	⌃
	try solve
	
	                    ^^^ *s*
	
	                              by nat π
	
	             ————————

//	*UK*
	Ger *can do lot togeth*
	
	           to meet ^^^ *s*
	
	             ————————

// *1.*	*EU*↗ ————————

a)   *50 yrs* | The chronology is important, so this is noted in the margin.

b)   *nat π*   *Π = policy.*
nat = *national*. We are not obliged to use symbols we have created if they do not leap immediately to mind or if they are not the quickest, clearest option. Here noting ▢ ^{al} for *national* would not have saved any time.

c)   ∧∧∧   The same symbol denotes two different, but fundamentally synonymous words (problem, challenge). Here the collocation will help us choose the right word during the production phase - *solve problem, meet challenge.*

d)   *can do lot*
togeth   This is not a very elegant way of noting, but sometimes, if nothing better comes to mind instantly, we just have to go with what we have!

Speech 4   MacShane 1

1.

I am delighted to be back here in Sofia. The first time I came to Bulgaria was 20 years ago and then I never dreamed I would return as a UK government minister.

Let me explain.

<table>
<tr><td rowspan="6">1st　*20 yrs* |

//</td><td>*☺*

here
————————</td></tr>
<tr><td>X *õ* |</td></tr>
<tr><td>∩</td></tr>
<tr><td>*rtn as Min* ○</td></tr>
<tr><td>————————

Explain</td></tr>
<tr><td>————————</td></tr>
</table>

a)　　☺　　　　You won't need to draw the eyes on your smiley (it's a waste of precious time) but this type font insists on them.

b)　　*here*　　　We know where here is, because if we are working consecutively we are there too! So we aren't going to note it!

c)　　*20 yrs* |　　The past tense symbol for a verb has been adapted to denote *ago*.

2.

In 1980 and 1981 I was heavily involved in supporting the independent Polish Union, Solidarność. In 1982 I was arrested and imprisoned in Warsaw when taking money to the underground activists of the union – men and women who today occupy high places in the national life of Poland. When I was released I was declared persona non grata by the communist government.

// 81-82	$\overline{}$ //
	s ( )
	_____
82	*arrest* / *imprison* / (*Warsaw*)
	money to activ o
	(*VIP s now*)
	_____
//	*release*
	persona non grata
	→
	_____

a) $\overline{}$ / Support. The vertical is holding up the horizontal part of the symbol. They do not meet, though, so that it is clearly different from the letter T.

b) *S* For anyone with any knowledge of Polish affairs *S* = Solidarność. If you aren't so familiar you may have to write it out.

c) *( )* General knowledge is enough to fill the brackets and add *independent Polish Union* for our audience who may not know.

d) *VIP s now* Noting the simple for the complicated. Since 1989 the former activists have become important figures, noted here with the English abbreviation *VIP* . The style, detail and register are easily added from memory.

3.

    I could not get a visa for Poland. My friends struggling for Polish freedom could not travel to the West. But we could both travel visa free to Varna. So on the sands of the Black Sea, the contacts were re-established, and over a glass of the wonderful wine that Bulgaria has the genius to produce, my footnote in the history of Europe's liberation from communism continued to be written.

→	*X visa*
+	*activ ^{o} s*
	X visa _____
B	*OK visa*
	to Varna _____
→	*recontact* *(wine !)*
+	*footnote !* ----------→
	_____

a)   *activ ^{o} s*   *activ ^{o}* = *activist*. The *s* denotes the plural, so we have *my friends struggling for Polish freedom*. Quicker, isn't it?

b)   →   *Therefore*. The result of being *persona non grata* is that he can't get a visa.

c)   (*wine !*)   This is such a vivid image that we will have no trouble recall this little compliment to our Bulgarian hosts. The exclamation mark serves to remind us of this image and that the language used is a little more flowery than usual.

d)   *footnote !*   An interesting choice of word by the speaker, and as such it will help memory to recreate the rest of the passage.

e)   ---------→   *Continue*

4.

Now I am glad to be back in Bulgaria as a new generation of Bulgarian and British European citizens prepare to shape a new Europe. I am especially pleased to be speaking to you under the auspices of the Atlantic Club. Tony Blair, Bill Clinton, my friend the NATO General Secretary George Robertson, Mikhail Gorbachev and the Dalai Lama have all spoken here.

||

☺

here
_____

Bulg
Brit   Eur °

prepare

to shape Eur.

_____

|| ☺

A C

_____

T B
Clinton
George Robertson
Gorby
Dalai Lama

___" | here

a) T B
    Clinton
    George Robertson
    Gorby
    Dalai Lama

Different types of abbreviations depending on how memorable the names and people are and how their names are usually abbreviated. The least well known are written in full.

b) A C

Atlantic Club. This would be a one-off abbreviation for this meeting. (See Part I Symbols, ii).

5.

It is an honour to follow in their footsteps, just as it is an honour to recall the memory of Major Frank Thompson, the poet and brother of one of England's greatest historians, E. P. Thompson. Frank Thompson parachuted into Bulgaria in 1944 as an SOE operative but was captured and executed.

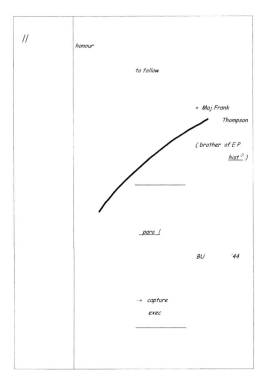

Figure 17

a)   *recall line*

Recall lines are particularly useful with proper names that are only used once or twice in a speech. They can be long and difficult to abbreviate.

6.

He sacrificed his life for Bulgaria and I recall his name tonight.

The Atlantic Club has of course played a key role in pushing Bulgaria towards NATO accession. As the date of accession draws ever closer,

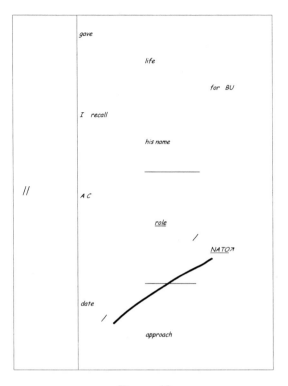

Figure 18

a)   *I recall*   Here we decide we want to be aware of the speaker's exact words, which we note.

b)   *NATO↗*   See also the symbol for EU enlargement (page 197)

7.

   I wonder however whether it is time for the Club to adopt a new slogan. The one in front of me/below me (on a banner, saying ,NATO Accession NOW!') seems so successful, it appears rather outdated. Perhaps it is time to consider something else? "A Functioning and Effective Judiciary NOW!" would go down well just now in Europe's capital, Brussels, but it doesn't quite have the same ring to it. I would offer a new slogan "Let's Europeanize the Balkans before we Balkanize Europe!"

?

// ?

new slogan ?

_____

old one

so success

→ outdated

_____

Time for

new slogan ?

_____

" funct ^{g} judiciary
effect now "

B	BXL s ♥ ^
	X catchy
	_____
I »	" Let 's
	Eur ^ze^
	Balkans
	b4
	Balkan ^ze^
	Eur "
	_____

a)   ? — The question mark in the margin shows that what follows is a question. This makes producing the correct intonation much easier.

b)   *outdated* — The interpreter has this banner in front of them with the slogan on it! And if it is written in 3 feet high letters in front of you, you won't need to note it down on your pad!

c)   ^ ♥ — *would like*

d)   *funct⁹ judiciary effect* — This is noted as fully as time will allow, as clearly being very close to the speaker's wording will be important here.

e)   " — Shows that this is a quote

2. Versions of the Tasks Set

Chapter 1   Speech Analysis

Speech writing guides (page 21)

Tonight we begin a new tradition for CPSR, presenting for the first time the Norbert Wiener Award for Social and Professional Responsibility [17]. It is especially fitting that we initiate it here at MIT, which was the intellectual home to Norbert Wiener for more than forty years[9].....

So we might think of Norbert Wiener as the patron saint of CPSR, although I suspect he would be a bit uncomfortable with the religious metaphor.

Tonight we are honoring a man who, like Wiener, might not fit the model of sainthood [10] but who, like Wiener, has served as a visible and inspiring example of social responsibility [2] [10]: David Lorge Parnas.[11]

David Parnas is Professor of Computer Science and Queen's University in Kingston, Ontario[2]. He received Bachelors, Masters, and Ph.D. degrees from the Carnegie Institute of Technology (now Carnegie Mellon University) and has taught at a number of prominent institutions in the United States, Germany, and Canada[2]. His research has been extremely influential in the field of software engineering, of which he can rightfully be called a founder[2]. He was one of the pioneers in work on structured programming, and his research still stands as a classic in that area[2].

On the basis of his work on making programming more productive and reliable, he was made head of the Software Engineering Research Section and director of the project on Software Cost Reduction at the Naval Research Laboratory, beginning in 1979. His expertise made him a natural choice to serve on the panel formed in 1985 to investigate the feasibility of the computing system required for the Strategic Defense Initiative ("Star Wars") program proposed by President Reagan[2] [10].

I do not need to rehearse[4] for this group the subsequent story (which Professor Parnas elaborated in his remarks on the panel discussion on ethics). To summarize quickly, he attended one meeting of the panel (now known as the Eastport Group) and recognized that the project was ill-conceived and unworkable[2] [10].

He raised his concerns with his colleagues on the panel, and although they could not refute his arguments, they saw the program as an opportunity to develop expanded research funding for computer science and did not want to hinder that bonanza (in which their own institutions would obviously share). After trying to take his concerns to the relevant government officials and failing to get their cooperation, he went public with a carefully written and cogent series of articles (later published in the Communications of the ACM and American Scientist) which still stand as the basic argument against the feasibility of SDI[10].

Structure maps (page 27)

Ladies and Gentlemen, Many thanks for inviting me here this evening. I have been asked to talk about "Germany and Britain: Meeting the Economic Challenge Together".	*What is he going to talk about?*
I think the "together" important. There is a great deal that we could do together and that we can learn from each other.	*Pros*
As you would expect, I shall paint a positive picture. But there is one aspect which causes some concern. To be provocative - I fear that Britain and Germany have somehow drifted apart.	
Not so much at government level, where quite the contrary has happened, as I'll explain in a minute. But at a personal level.	*and one problem*
Twenty years ago, German was a major language in British schools and many school children would visit Germany on regular exchanges. Spanish has now overtaken German, and young people in Britain have less exposure to Germany as a result.	*example 1 of problem*
The BAOR (British Army of the Rhine) was in those days some 65,000 strong. If you include families, relatives etc, that gave many more thousand British people reason to visit Germany. The army is now around 20,000: so again a fall off.	*example 2 of problem*
This ties in with another persistent element in our bilateral relationship: the image of Germany in Britain. I was looking recently at a survey of young people's attitudes in both countries.	
Germans see the UK as a good place to work and to study - second only to the US. They recognise that we have a creative, multicultural society.	*German view of UK*
But Germans see us as reluctant Europeans. They have the impression that we don't like them very much.	
Young British people said they admired Germany's high-quality cars and its well-organised people. But they still associated Germany with the 12 years between 1933	*UK view of Germany*

| and 1945. They thought Germans lacked a sense of humour and - astoundingly, since we always seem to lose to Germany - that they played bad football. | |

Mini-summaries (page 30)

For those of you who don't know me, I'm the Minister of Energy, Science, Fisheries and a few other things including climate change policy. It's that last one that has taken me up close and personal with dairy farmers and brought me the invitation to speak here today.	*Minister for things including Climate Change...*
So let's talk about the weather.	
I'm not about to tell you that the storms we're going through now are the result of climate change. I'm not a climatologist and I don't think even a climatologist would offer any conclusions on that score.	*Climate change not cause of today's bad weather*
But what I will tell you – and what a climatologist would tell you – is that this is what climate change looks like. One of the significant consequences expected from climate change is an increase in the frequency and severity of extreme weather events.	*But will cause future bad weather, very bad.*
This is why we use the term climate change in preference to global warming, because it more accurately captures the range of climatic effects that the enhanced greenhouse effect is expected to produce. A long-term increase in global average temperatures is the key indicator and consequence of the build-up of greenhouse gases in the Earth's atmosphere. But the expected effects of that change on the world's climate systems are multiple and diverse.	*"climate change" more accurate than "global warming"*
The New Zealand dairy industry is founded on the superb conditions this country's climate provides for growing grass. This is why climate change matters to dairy farmers and – because of the economic importance of your industry – to New Zealand.	*NZ's climate ideal for dairy farmers*

<table>
<tr>
<td>

We know climate change is already under way on a global scale and there do appear to be some measurable effects emerging in New Zealand. A study done for the Ministry for the Environment said a southward shift in subtropical pasture species might be one indicator, along with an increased frequency of warmer winters in recent decades. It also suggested that a recorded halving of the planted area in kiwifruit in Northland over the six years to 2001 could be at least partly attributable to a warming climate, leading to reduced productivity

</td>
<td>

Climate change started.

Study shows
1. species moving south
2. warmer winters

3. less kiwi fruit

</td>
</tr>
</table>

Chapter 2   Recognizing and Splitting Ideas (page 40)

To help, as well as splitting the text into ideas or SVO groups, I have also indicated the SVO structure in the first part of the speech.

S V
I am delighted to be back here in Sofia.

       S   V   O
The first time **I came to Bulgaria** was 20 years ago

     S   V
and then **I never dreamed** I would return as a UK government minister.

Let me explain.

        S   V
In 1980 and 1981 **I was** heavily involved in **supporting** the independent
                  O
Polish Union, **Solidarność**.

     S   V   V
In 1982 **I was arrested** and **imprisoned** in Warsaw when taking money to the underground activists of the union – men and women who today occupy high places in the national life of Poland.

            S   V   O
When I was released **I was declared persona non grata** by the communist government.

```
S      V      O
```
I could **not get** a **visa** for Poland.

```
          S                                    V                    O
```
My **friends** struggling for Polish freedom **could not travel** to the **West**.

```
        S              V            O
```
But **we** could both **travel** visa free **to Varna**.

```
                                              S          V
```
So on the sands of the Black Sea, the **contacts were re-established**,
and over a glass of the wonderful wine that Bulgaria has the genius to produce,

```
        S
```
my footnote in the history of Europe's liberation from communism

```
                V
```
continued to **be written**.

```
        S  V O
```
Now **I am glad** to be back in Bulgaria as a new generation of Bulgarian and British
European citizens prepare to shape a new Europe.

```
S  V              O
```
I am especially **pleased** to be speaking to you under the auspices of the Atlantic Club.

```
        S          S                                    S
```
Tony Blair, Bill Clinton, my friend the NATO General Secretary George

```
        S                              S          V      O
```
Robertson, Mikhail Gorbachev and the Dalai Lama have all **spoken** here.

```
S V      O
```
It is an honour to follow in their footsteps,

just as **it is an honour** to recall the memory of Major Frank Thompson, the poet and
brother of one of England's greatest historians, E P Thompson.

Frank Thompson parachuted into Bulgaria in 1944 as an SOE operative

but was captured and executed.

He sacrificed his life for Bulgaria

and I recall his name tonight.

The Atlantic Club has of course played a key role in pushing Bulgaria towards NATO
accession.

As the date of accession draws ever closer, I wonder however whether it is time for the
Club to adopt a new slogan.

The one in front of me/below me (on a banner, saying 'NATO Accession NOW!') seems so successful, it appears rather outdated.

Perhaps it is time to consider something else?

'A Functioning and Effective Judiciary NOW!' would go down well just now in Europe's capital, Brussels,

but it doesn't quite have the same ring to it.

I would offer a new slogan 'Let's Europeanize the Balkans before we Balkanize Europe!'

Because the story of Europe in the lifetime of Europeans born since the end of the Second World War is little short of amazing.

Our parents and grandparents grew up in a Europe that knew mainly violence, repression, emigration, religious intolerance and grinding poverty.

For too many Europeans, life was nasty, brutish and short of nearly everything today's European Union guarantees its citizens.

To be sure, a European elite enjoyed high art, great literature and the chance to shine as officers on the field, gentlemen of the court, men of money or professors in the academy.

But from 500 BC when the term Europe was first used - Europa was actually a maiden taken to the shores of Turkey to be ravished - until 1989, our continent failed rather than provided for its peoples.

And today? The changes, even since 1973, when Britain entered the European Economic Community, are remarkable:

The Europe of 1973 with its border control on goods and cars has gone.

The myriad of currencies and currency controls acting as a blockage to fair, transparent, effective business has been replaced by a single market. One where the majority of EU citizens sensibly use one currency - the Euro.

The Europe of 1973 with dirty beaches, and expensive air travel and telephone calls has been replaced by a Europe which allows more people to travel, talk to each other and enjoy a shared and better-protected natural environment than ever before.

But perhaps most importantly, the division of the Europe of 1973 into communist, fascistic and democratic zones has all but disappeared.

For the first time in European history a century opens up in which war, hunger, political oppression and fear are not the lot of the majority of European citizens.

Europe has come a long way.

But now is not the time to look back and marvel at what we have achieved.

We need to look forward: beyond the fifteen current Member States and beyond even the ten countries joining the EU next May.

Our primary objective should be to make sure that Europeans across the continent share in this progress.

This means making a success of the first wave of accession in 2004.

But equally importantly, it means maintaining the momentum of the process
and looking ahead to the next milestone - and Bulgaria's accession together with Romania in 2007.

Note that the S V O groups in this speech vary from 3 to 41 words in length.

Chapter 4   Links

Step 1 (page 58)

> You all know that the British Government would like to join the euro once the five economic tests are met.
>
> **But** selling the decision to the British public in a referendum will be difficult,
>
> **if** the eurozone economies, with Germany at the head, are seen to be performing badly.
>
> **If** on the other hand they are undertaking structural reforms which are dealing with the problems they face,
>
> **[then]** promoting the euro in the UK is a much easier task.

NB The "if" clause can come before AND after its partner clause, as we can see here.

Step 5 (page 63)

//	I don't believe that common rules across the EU are a solution to everything.
//	Different countries have different systems and structures,
→	**so** a solution which works in one place will not necessarily work in another.
//	It doesn't make sense to regulate everything from Brussels.
B	**But** it does make sense to share our experience and to learn from each other.
eg	Look **for example** at Germany and Britain.
//	In Britain we envy Germany's training system for example. Or the high productivity of its workers.
→	[so] We can learn from Germany's successes here.

//	And in Britain we have had successes too.
eg	[**e.g.**] Getting the long term unemployed back into work has been a major success

NB In the square brackets *so* and *e.g.* were not actually said by the speaker, but are implied by them and so we note them.

Step 6 (page 64)

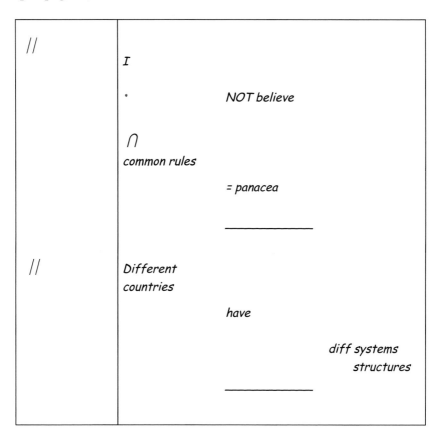

$\rightarrow$ solution

                              may work

                                                        in   A
                                                        not   B

                                          _____

|| regulate all

                              NOT make sense

                                          _____

B   sharing experience
          + learning

                                          DOES make sense

                                          _____

eg   DE + UK

                                          _____

//	UK
	envy
	DE training
	+ productivity
	_____
→	UK
	can learn
	_____

//	UK
	also has
	successes
	_____
eg	long term unemploy

Chapter 5   Verticality and Hierarchies of Values

Parallel values (page 82)

//	*bus* [ns] *trade* + *terrorism* _____

//	*I*
	
	   express
	
	      solidarity
	    _____

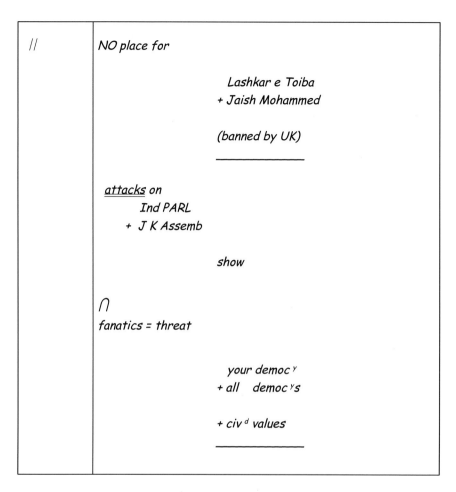

Please note that no attempt has been made to note every detail here but only to demonstrate the ideas described in this chapter.

Shifting values (page 86)

partly COS	*history*
	————————
	history
	gives
	<u>*advantage*</u>
	? unparalleled ?
	————————

We	*allies* / *US*
	————————
We	*EU*
	————————
Our ties	*Commonwealth* *India* *Sub Continent*
	strengthening
	————————

Here I have shifted the *we* and *our* to the left for emphasis.

AND
 	
our relations
      /
	
	Mid East
	Russia
	China
	                    closer
	                    ‾‾‾‾‾‾‾‾‾‾

Parallel values 2 (page 90)

//	*Rules*
	          = *tough*
	          ‾‾‾‾‾‾‾‾‾‾
	
	     require
	
	                              open markets
	                              (painful)
	          ‾‾‾‾‾‾‾‾‾‾
	
	     require
	
	∩ *politicians*
	          invest

tho	*benefits*
	
	           come
	
	                      after elections
	           _____

Use of brackets (page 97)

→	*issues*
	
	                affect
	                          continents
	
	                          (X countries)
	           _____
	
	working at Eur level
	
	           = *only way*
	
	           (for MS
	                + future MS)
	           _____

|| *collectively*

we

will benefit

vast market

(bigger than US + JAPAN)

_____

3.   The Examples

Below is a list of the speeches used as examples and Internet addresses at which they can be found. In **bold** is the abbreviated reference to each speech used in Parts I-III, e.g. **Blair 2**. It is inevitable that with time the original URLs will no longer be valid. In order to ensure that you will still have access when this occurs, the texts have also been made available at this address.

http://interpreters.free.fr/shortcourse/examplesmenu.htm

1   Moskow

This is a speech by Michael H. Moskow, President of the Federal Reserve Bank of Chicago, given to the 39th Annual Conference on Bank Structure and Competition, at the Fairmont Hotel in Chicago on May 8th 2003. In it Mr Moskow introduces Alan Greenspan, Chairman of the Federal Reserve System, the US Central Bank, as guest speaker to the assembled bankers. Mr Greenspan will speak via video-link. The conference deals with the subject of corporate governance and takes place amid a number of scandals highlighting the failure of the same in the U.S. Mr Moskow refers to this in his introduction.

http://www.chicagofed.org/news_and_conferences/speeches/2003_05_08.cfm

2   Winograd

These remarks were made by the President of the organization Computer Professionals for Corporate Responsibility (CPSR), Terry Winograd, upon presentation of the first Norbert Wiener Award for Social and Professional Responsibility. Norbert Wiener is held by CPSR to have laid the foundations for many aspects of modern computing, as well as being a leader in assessing the social implications of that new and emerging technology. For this reason a prize in his name is awarded by CPSR for outstanding contributions in the field of Corporate Social Responsibility. Norbert Wiener died in 1964. The award is made to Professor David Lorge Parnas. The speech is made after a dinner, held for several hundred people.

http://www.cpsr.org/cpsr/wiener-speech.html

3   Blair 1

 Speech given by Tony Blair, Prime Minister of UK on measures to combat anti-social behaviour. Mr Blair is speaking on 14th October at Queen Elizabeth

II Conference Centre, London to an audience of police officers from around the country. Its topic is the introduction of new legal measures to curb anti-social behaviour, particularly in young people, an issue that has been given a lot of press coverage in the months prior to the speech.

http://www.number-10.gov.uk/output/Page4644.asp

4   Buzek

In this speech the then Polish Prime Minister, Jerzy Buzek, introduces a debate on European integration. The debate takes place against the backdrop of Poland's accession negotiations which must be concluded speedily if Poland is to join the EU as planned. (At this time that date was still 1st January 2003). The speech was given in the Polish Parliament, the Sejm, in the first quarter of 2000.

http://ks.sejm.gov.pl:8009/forms/kad.htm

5   Torry 1

British Ambassador, Sir Peter Torry is speaking on 20th January 2004 at a function of the British Chamber of Commerce in Germany, at Duesseldorf Industrie Club. He had been in his post 6 months at the time and was speaking to an audience of around 300 business people, some of whom had the opportunity to put questions afterwards.

http://www.britischebotschaft.de/en/news/items/040115.htm

6   Hodgson

This speech was delivered by New Zealand government Minister, Pete Hodgson, on 19th February 2004 to an audience of New Zealand dairy farmers at the Dairy Expo 2004, in the TSB Stadium, New Plymouth, New Zealand. The title of the speech was, "Why climate change matters". Although global warming may not affect New Zealand as much as other countries new Zealand has been hit by damage to the ozone layer, so the public is sensitive to climate issues. Also this audience of farmers will have a vested interest in any, even minor changes to the climate.

http://www.climatechange.govt.nz/resources/speeches.html

7   Torry 2

This speech was given by Sir Peter Torry, British Ambassador to Germany, in Hamburg, 24th July 2003, the 60th Anniversary of the British bombing of Hamburg during the Second World War. He is speaking to a predominantly German audience and tries to focus on the positive elements linking Hamburg and the UK rather than on wartime events. As ambassador one of his jobs is to maintain good relations between the UK and Germany.

http://www.britischebotschaft.de/en/news/items/030724.htm

8   Patten

A speech given by Chris Patten, then European Commissioner for External Relations, to the plenary session of the European Parliament on July 3rd 2000. He is reporting on the European Council of Ministers summit in Feira, Portugal, a few days earlier. In this extract he is speaking about relations with Russia.

http://www3.europarl.eu.int/omk/omnsapir.so/debatsL5?FILE= 20000703EN&LANGUE=EN&LEVEL=DOC&NUMINT=1- 058&SEARCH=ORAT&LEG=L5

9   MacShane 1

This is a speech given by Denis MacShane, UK Minister for Europe on 8th October 2003 at the Atlantic Club in Sofia, Bulgaria. The Atlantic Club is a non-governmental organization which supported NATO accession for Bulgaria and fosters Euro-Atlantic values. Denis MacShane's parents are Polish emigrés, he speaks Polish and made many trips to Poland before and after the events of 1989. He is speaking in the context of Bulgaria's attempts to join the EU and after Bulgaria's accession to NATO.

http://www.fco.gov.uk/servlet/Front?pagename=OpenMarket/Xcelerate/ShowP age&c=Page&cid=1007029391647&a=KArticle&aid=1065714328868

10   Blair 2

This speech was given by the British Prime Minister, Tony Blair, to the Confederation of Indian Industry, on 5th January 2002, in Bangalore, India. Bangalore is the motor of the Indian high-tech industry. The war on terror has begun and India has its own problems of violence in Kashmir as well as with tensions between Hindu nationalists and India's Muslim minority.

http://www.infy.com/media/BritishPMSpeech.pdf

11   MacShane 2

Denis MacShane in Bucharest, Romania. The title of the speech is "Romania and Britain: sharing a new partnership in a new Europe" and it was delivered on 7th October 2003. Mr MacShane is in Romania talking about accession to the

EU and problems that Romania, the UK and Europe face. His own parents are Polish emigrés, he speaks Polish and made many trips to Poland before and after the events of 1989. He is not therefore a complete beginner in Eastern European affairs.

http://www.fco.gov.uk/servlet/Front?pagename=OpenMarket/Xcelerate/ShowPage&c=Page&cid=1007029391647&a=KArticle&aid=1065714309775

12   Whitty

Speech held by Lord Whitty of Camberwell, Minister for Farming, Food and Sustainable Energy, at the 5th British-German Environment Forum in Berlin, on 5th February 2004. The Germans remember are much greener than the Brits.

http://www.britischebotschaft.de/en/news/items/040205b.htm

13   Reid

John Reid MP, Secretary of State for Health in UK, 28th April 2004. The title of the speech is 'Choosing health - closing the gap on inequalities'. Mr Reid is talking to health professionals from the National Health Service about reforms to the service aimed at ensuring equal access to health services for all.

http://www.dh.gov.uk/NewsHome/Speeches/SpeechesList/SpeechesArticle/fs/en?CONTENT_ID=4081307&chk=96zwcE

4. Where to Find Practice Material

When looking for practice material remember to follow the guidelines in the Introduction. That is to say, look for speeches that might have been interpreted consecutively or which were given in situations where consecutive might have been used.

In addition to the suggestions made in the introduction you could try typing a few key words into your favourite search engine and see what you come up with. For example, typing "*speech*" and "*minister*" and "*climate change*" into Google in late 2004 returns ministerial speeches from ministers of the UK, Canada and Germany among the first ten results alone. The same will work for all sorts of different types of speeches and speakers and of course in any language. Just explore!

English

The British Embassy in Berlin.
>   http://www.britischebotschaft.de/en/
UK Department of Trade and Industry.
>   http://www.dti.gov.uk/ministers/speeches/
UK Foreign Office
>   http://www.fco.gov.uk
UK Prime Minister's Office
>   http://www.number-10.gov.uk/

French

This site, called *Collection de discours publiques,* is a fantastic archive of French political discourse. Just enter the name of a speaker or a subject and you will never be short of practice material again.

http://discours-publics.ladocumentationfrancaise.fr/rechlogos/servlet/
RechServlet?_page=ACCUEIL&_type=NEW

Polish

Speeches by the Polish President
http://www.msz.gov.pl/file_libraries/31/333/0110.doc
http://www.prezydent.pl/pre/index.php3

General

The site at which the example speeches for this book have been made available also offers more practice material:
Interpreter Training Resources website:
     http://interpreters.free.fr/links/practicematerial.htm

Remember, there are many more sources out there than we have space for here.

Glossary

Automatization   See internalization.

Bottom-up   To learn about the process by starting with the result rather than vice
                      versa. Here this means using a note-taking system to help learn how
                      to analyse a source speech, rather than using speech analysis to create
                      notes.

Concept   The underlying meaning of a word or more often several synonymous
                      words, e.g. propose, suggest, put forward,

In consecutive   Another way of saying consecutive interpreting, as opposed to
mode   simultaneous interpreting.

Hierarchy   The order of importance of the elements noted should be visible in the
                      way the notes arranged on the page.

Idea   That which is expressed by a Subject Verb Object group.

Internalization   The process of learning to complete a task successfully so that that
                      task can be carried out without having to think about doing it. Also
                      called automatization. Requires very little theoretical knowledge and
                      lots of practice.

Links   In purely grammatical terms these are usually conjunctions. They are
                      words and expressions which describe the relation between two ideas.

Macro-thinking /   Looking at the bigger picture of how a speech is built up rather than
macro-approach   just the words and sentences. For example, identifying the function a
                      part of a speech fulfils.

Margin   A column of 2 or 3 cm at the left of the page, bordered by a vertical
                      line, in which the interpreter can note elements of particular
                      importance.

Mind map	A way of organizing information on a piece of paper. Typically an organic chart (can be multi-coloured) laid out on a large sheet of paper. It contains words and drawings that are connected to one another in various ways. By tapping into the way the mind associates and recalls information it helps us organize and remember information.
Mini-summary	A very brief summary of a speech, where each section of the whole is described in just a few words.
Mother tongue	An interpreter's best active language, independently of whether it is the language of either of their parents or even of their country of birth. In exceptional cases an interpreter may have two mother tongues. (Jones, 2002:131)
Multi-tasking	Doing several things at once.
Notepad	Usually, but not exclusively, a reporter's notepad of 10 x 15 cm on which interpreters make notes when working in consecutive mode.
Organic forms	One basic form, often a symbol, which, through the addition of other elements, gives rise to a whole family of related symbols.
Parallel values	Two elements of a passage which carry equal weight in the speaker's mind and delivery are noted parallel to one another on the page in order to highlight this equivalence.
Production phase	In the whole process that is consecutive interpreting this is when the interpreter is speaking to their audience; using their notes to recreate their version of a source speech.
Pro-forms	For our purposes, an expression that refers back, not to one person, or object, but to a whole passage, a whole idea, or series of events.
Recall line	If a concept is repeated in quick succession so that the interpreter will note it twice on the same page or on successive pages it may be quicker to draw a line from the first notation of the concept to the place it would have appeared the second time rather than rewrite the word or redraw the symbol.
Shifting values	Placing elements in your notes according to their importance to one another. The more important something is the further to the left it will appear on the page.
Source language	The language of the speech which you are reading or listening to, and which you are going to interpret from into another language.

Source text/ speech	The speech (in its written or spoken form) from which we take notes in Chapters 1-4 and which we interpret consecutively from in Chapter 5 onwards.
Structure map	A summary description of the function and/or framework of a speech's component parts, rather than of its content.
SVO	Subject Verb Object. The basic word order of most Indo-European languages. (Although many languages have a certain flexibility in respect of word order, like German or the Slavic languages, the starting point is still SVO.)
Symbol	Any mark in your notes, be it a picture, short word or single letter, which represents a concept.
Target language	The language into which you are going to interpret a source text.
Tiering	A synonym for verticality.
Transcode	A term that you wish to transfer from the source language into your target language version in order to be sure to be faithful to the speaker's message. The transcoded term will be pronounced and used as thought it were a correct term in the target language although, strictly speaking, it may not be.
Version at the back	This means a version, and does NOT mean the only correct version.
Verticality	The technique of noting from top to bottom on the page rather than from left to right. First described by Rozan (1956). Also called tiering.
Written texts	The written record of a speech that has been delivered orally in public by the speaker, transcript.

Further Reading

Note-taking in consecutive interpreting is really something that you should practise a lot, rather than read too much about, but here is a brief selection of titles that may be of use to student interpreters wishing to improve their note-taking technique for consecutive interpreting.

Gillies, Andrew (2004) *Conference Interpreting - A New Students' Companion*. Cracow: Tertium.
A compilation of practice exercises for student interpreters for various component skills of conference interpreting, including note-taking for consecutive interpreting. Second revised and expanded edition of a book first published in 2001.

Jones, Roderick (2002) *Conference Interpreting Explained*, Manchester: St Jerome.
The single most useful book about interpreting you can read with very clear and helpful sections on consecutive interpreting and note-taking for consecutive interpreting. Second edition of a book first published in 1998.

Monacelli, Claudia (1999) *Messaggi in codice. Analisi del discorso e strategie per prenderne appunti*, Milan: FrancoAngeli.
Lots of really interesting strategies for tackling speeches and creating notes. Includes mind-mapping and lots of examples of real notes.

Rozan , J-F. (1956) *La prise de notes en interprétation consécutive*, Genève: Georg. [English translation by Andrew Gillies (2003) *Note-taking in Consecutive Interpreting*, Cracow: Tertium]
The original and still undisputed champion of books on note-taking. Very brief and very clear, this classic is now available in English as well.

References

Ahrens, Barbara (2003) "Hieroglyphen auf dem Block—Über den Nutzen der Symbole beim Notieren", *Mitteilungsblatt für Dolmetscher und Übersetzer* 49: 3–4.

Alexieva, Bistra (1994) "On teaching note-taking in consecutive interpreting", in Cay Dollerup and Annette Lindegaard (eds), *Teaching Translation and Interpreting 2: Insight, Aims, Visions,* Amsterdam and Philadelphia: John Benjamins, 199-206.

------ (1998) "Consecutive Interpreting as a Decision Process", in Ann Beylard-Ozeroff, Jana Kralova and Barbara Moser-Mercer (eds), *Translators' Strategies and Creativity*, Amsterdam and Philadelphia: John Benjamins, 181-189.

Allioni, Sergio (1989) "Towards a Grammar of Consecutive Interpretation", in Laura Gran and John Dodds (eds), 191-199.

Andres, Doerte (2000) *Konsekutivdolmetschen und Notation,* Mainz: FASK.

Baker, Mona (1992) *In Other Words*, London: Routledge.

Ballester, Ana and Catalina Jimenez (1992) "Approaches to the teaching of interpreting: mnemonic and analytic strategies", in Cay Dollerup and Anne Loddegard (eds) *Teaching translation and interpreting: Training, Talent and Experience*, Amsterdam and Philadelphia: John Benjamins, 237-244.

Garzone, G., F. Santulli and D. Damiani (1990) *LA "TERZA" LINGUA - metodo di stesura degli appunti e traduzione consecutiva*, Milan: Istituto Editoriale Universitario.

Garretson, Deborah. (1981) "A Psychological Approach to Consecutive Interpretation", *Meta:* XXVI, 3: 244-254..

Gile, Daniel (1995) *Basic Concepts and Models for Interpreter and Translator training*, Amsterdam and Philadelphia: John Benjamins.

------ (1999) "Testing the effort model's tightrope hypothesis in simultaneous interpreting – a contribution". *Hermes Journal of Linguistics* No. 23: 153-172.

Gillies, Andrew (2002) 'Zastosowanie osiągnięć współczesnej dydaktyki w szkoleniu tłumaczy konferencyjnych'. [The application of contemporary teaching methodology in the training of conference interpreters], in *Język trzeciego tysiąclecia II*, Cracow: Tertium, 215-226.

------ (2004) *Conference Interpreting - A New Students' Companion*. Cracow: Tertium, 2nd edition.

Gran, Laura and John Dodds (eds) (1989) *The Theoretical and Practical Aspects of Teaching Conference Interpreting*, Udine: Campanotto Editore.

Heine, Manfred (2000) "Effektives Selbststudium – Schluessel zum Erfolg in der Dolmetscherausbildung", in Sylvia Kalina, Silke Buhl and Heidrun Arbogast (eds) *Dolmetschen : Theorie – Praxis – Didaktik*, Saarbruecken: Roehriger UniVerlag, 213-229.

Jones, Roderick (2002) *Conference Interpreting Explained*, Manchester: St Jerome, 2nd edition.

Lorayne, Harry. (1958) *How to Develop a Superpowered Memory*, Preston: A.Thomas.

Margolis Frederic and Chip R. Bell (1986) *Instructing for Results*, Minnesota: Pfeiffer.

Mackintosh, Jennifer. (1999) "Interpreters are made not born", *Interpreting* 4.1: 67-80.

Matyssek, Heinz (1989) *Handbuch der Notizentechnik fuer Dolmetscher*, Heidelberg: Julius Gross Verlag.

Monacelli, Claudia (1999) *Messaggi in codice. Analisi del discorso e strategie per prenderne appunti*, Milan: FrancoAngeli.

Neff, Jacquy (1989) "Pour une méthologie dans l'enseignement de l'interprétation consécutive", in Laura Gran and John Dodds (eds), 229-235.

Perlman, Alan (1998) *Writing Great Speeches*, Boston: Allyn and Bacon.

Rozan, Jean-François. (1956) *La prise de notes en interprétation consécutive*, Geneva: Georg; trans. by Andrew Gillies as *Note-taking in Consecutive Interpreting* (2003), Cracow: Tertium.

Sayeg, Yuki (1992) "Note-taking for beginners", *Forum*: Issue 12: 1-2.

Seleskovitch, Danica (1968) *L'interprète dans les conferences internationales*, Paris: Lettres Modernes, Minard.

Seleskovitch, Danica (1975) *Langage, Langue et memoire*, Paris: Lettres Modernes, Minard.

Seleskovitch, Danica and Marianne Lederer (2002) *Pédagogie raisonnée de l'interprétation,* Paris: Didier Erudition, 2nd edition.

Szabo, Csilla (ed) (2003) *Interpreting: From Preparation to Performance*, Budapest: British Council.

Taylor, Christopher (1989) "Textual Memory and the Teaching of Consecutive Interpretation", in Laura Gran and John Dodds (eds), 177-184.

Taylor-Bouladon, Valerie (2001) *Conference Interpreting – Principles and Practice*, Adelaide: Crawford House.

Thierry, Christopher (1981) "L'enseignement de la prise de notes en interprétation consécutive: un faux problème?", in Jean Delisle, *L'enseignement de l'interprétation et de la traduction - de la theorie a la pédagogie. Cahiers de traductologie 4*, Ottawa: 99-112.

------ (1989) "Pédagogie de l'example dans l'enseignement de l'interprétation simultanée et consécutive", in Laura Gran and John Dodds (eds), 207-209.

Van Dam, Helle (2004) "Interpreters' notes - On the choice of language", *Interpreting* 6.1: 3-17.

Weber, W. (1989) "Improved Ways of Teaching Consecutive Interpretation", in Laura Gran and John Dodds (eds), 161-166.

Zalka, I. (1989) "The Teaching of Lexical Items in Consecutive Interpretation", in Laura Gran and John Dodds (eds), 185-189.

INDEX